Rosemary
and
Bitter Oranges

GROWING UP IN A TUSCAN KITCHEN

Patrizia Chen

SCRIBNER

New York   London   Toronto   Sydney   Singapore

SCRIBNER
1230 Avenue of the Americas
New York, NY 10020

SCRIBNER and design are trademarks of Macmillan Library Reference USA, Inc.,
used under license by Simon & Schuster, the publisher of this work.
For information regarding special discounts for bulk purchases,
please contact Simon & Schuster Special Sales at 1-800-456-6798 or
business@simonandschuster.com

DESIGNED BY KYOKO WATANABE

Set in Apollo

Manufactured in the United States of America

1 3 5 7 9 10 8 6 4 2

Library of Congress Cataloging-in-Publication Data
Chen, Patrizia.
Rosemary and bitter oranges : growing up in a Tuscan kitchen / Patrizia Chen.
p. cm.
1. Cookery, Italian—Tuscan style. I. Title.

TX723.2.T86 C46 2003
641.5945'5—dc21   2002036460

ISBN 978-1-4165-7526-9

To Lydia,

who said,

"You can do it."

CONTENTS

Contents

Contents

Rosemary
and
Bitter Oranges

EMILIA

Emilia in front of the kitchen door

I grew up in Livorno, a boisterous town in Tuscany. In Livorno, the flavors of food, the colors of nature, and the scent of the pittosporum bushes along the *passeggiata a mare,* the beautiful promenade along the sea, are bolder and less domesticated than anywhere else in elegant Tuscany.

The nonaristocratic beginnings of my natal town have chiseled a certain expression on its people's faces and marked their vernacular with a wit that lashes out and leaves a mark. The word that describes our most characteristic traits is *beceri* (boorish), and the Livornesi have almost managed to convert this admittedly insulting adjective, used strictly in Tuscany, into a term of affection. Yes, loud and boorish we definitely are, and we take pride in the countless tales of pirates and brigands indissolubly linked to our history.

I lived for a great part of my childhood with my parents and grandparents in a big three-story house. My parents always ate downstairs at the table in the dining room with my grandparents, Nonno GianPaolo and Nonna Valentina. My brother, my sisters, and I were supposed to take our meals upstairs. The exclusion from the adults' table itself was enough to make me wish to be part of their evening ritual, even if it meant only being allowed to say two phrases during the entire meal: *"Grazie," "No grazie."* The few times we were allowed to dine downstairs, flawless dishes would be brought in by Emilia, our beloved cook, who bustled unperturbed between her stove and the dining room. The food was invariably white—uniformly white—and bland. Always very good, always impeccably executed, but so bland. Many soufflés, lots of *sformati* (timbales), *paste al gratin,* and beautiful fish— maybe a *merluzzo* (a small Mediterranean cod), steamed to perfection, with a whisper of extra-virgin olive oil. Food was judged by the same standard as fashion: spiciness was as vulgar as a skintight dress.

One day as I passed through the kitchen after playing in the garden, my senses were suddenly awakened, stirred by a vivid aroma that I had never experienced at the table with my family. Emilia was eating the meal she had prepared for herself. It was an explosion of colors: vermilion tomatoes, green *basilico* and parsley, and contrasting black pepper dots. And the smell! Pungent, strong, and exotic enough to stop me, and my seven-year-old nose, in my tracks.

Emilia must have recognized a soul mate in my startled, hungry look. *"Vuoi provare?"* She scooped up some of that wonderful redness with a big morsel of bread and offered it to me. "Oh, Emilia!" I gushed. "This is so tasty." I had finally discovered real food, and I was hooked forever. Now I knew that life—real life—happened behind the kitchen doors and not in the subdued, elegant atmosphere of my grandparents' dining room.

Having shared her food with me, Emilia went a step further and offered to give me cooking lessons. I eagerly accepted.

Emilia was a fierce, thickset woman, one of many siblings born in a small fishing village a few kilometers south of Livorno. Sent to work at a very early age—as was the custom at the time—she had come to the big city in search of a good job and somehow landed in our home, becoming a constant presence in our life. Emilia had been there for us children since our births.

At the start of our afternoons together, Emilia enveloped me tightly in the blue-and-white-striped apron that would protect my clothes. She carefully rolled up the sleeves of my dresses and sweaters to avoid likely disasters and showed me how to wash my hands thoroughly, scrubbing fingertips and nails with ruthless vigor. Only after she was satisfied that the garden grime had been scoured from my arms, hands, and fingertips did she allow me to dip a spoon into a dish of flour or to help her knead dough.

Emilia asserted that a good cook had to be able to handle the range of more disgusting chores, and I obeyed wholeheartedly. *"Attenta, Bimba!* Be careful not to leave any trace of bile, or the chicken will be unbearably bitter. Look inside the stomach and scrub it meticulously; the bile is dark and easy to spot," Emilia cautioned. The tiny brown livers had to be put aside for future gourmet usage. I gingerly played with their spongy consistency, examining the white filaments that enshrouded them like a fishnet. Within hours they would end up in delicate ragù sauces or— mixed with veal and prosciutto—become a delicious filling for the little *vols-au-vent* often served as appetizers.

Inserting my fingers into the gills and guts of fish and poultry were all part of my formal kitchen education. I learned to scale fish, standing on a stool in front of the gray marble counter, and instantly took to this particular task. The messiness of sending millions of translucent, silvery scales flying all over the sink and onto the kitchen floor fitted beautifully with my innate love for visual anarchy. I quickly learned the secrets of sending to the *tavola dei Signori* the perfectly elegant *sformati* while savoring the conspiratorial joy of producing strong, lush sauces to complement spaghetti, polenta, meats, and fish for just Emilia and me. We prepared thick ragùs with veal, sausages, and prosciutto. We sautéed the dark leaves of *cavolo nero* (Tuscan black cabbage) in olive oil, red pepper, and lots of garlic. I no longer yearned to sit at the adults' table; my meals with Emilia were far better!

Herbs were an essential part of Emilia's cooking, though not all of them were destined for my grandparents' table. Oregano, which has to be used in small quantities to avoid prevailing over other savors, was an important and acceptable addition. She sent me to the garden to pick what she needed for both my grandparents and herself: basil and parsley from the pots immediately outside the kitchen door, the other herbs from the patch near the chicken pen, where a few bushes of rosemary and sage grew tall and lopsided under the old medlar tree. I learned the characteristics and value of particular spices when she taught me her favorite dishes, the food from her family tradition. I learned to love the spiciness of *peperoncino rosso,* the strong red pepper from Campania, in the south of Italy, and the pungent bite of the black peppercorns she crushed into meat and fish.

✁ *Salsa di Pomodoro d'Emilia* ✁
EMILIA'S TOMATO SAUCE

Emilia would add a sprig of basil or rosemary or a glass of red wine along with the tomatoes, according to her mood. The sauce always turned out a bit differently, yet it was always delicious.

1 medium yellow onion
1 medium carrot
1 clove garlic
½ stalk celery
2 tablespoons extra-virgin olive oil
1 pound ripe tomatoes or one 14-ounce can crushed
    tomatoes
Pinch of red pepper flakes (optional)
Salt and freshly ground pepper *a piacere* (to taste)

Peel and finely chop the onion, carrot, and garlic. Finely chop the celery. Sauté the vegetables in the olive oil in a medium saucepan over low heat, stirring, until they begin to soften, about 5 minutes.

Meanwhile, if using fresh tomatoes, peel and seed them, then roughly chop.

Stir the fresh or canned tomatoes into the vegetables. For extra zing, add some red pepper flakes. Simmer gently for 2 hours, stirring occasionally, until the sauce is thick and flavorful. Season with salt and pepper.

Makes about 2 cups

The kitchen in my grandparents' house was larger than the dining room and opened directly onto the garden. Tall French doors with imposing green shutters led to a small semienclosed patio full of plants and Emilia's household implements. An upside-down shabby millet broom, a scrubbing brush, and a pail—on top of which a dingy scouring cloth was laid to dry—rested in a corner. A proletarian gray stone terrace on the kitchen side marked the boundary of Emilia's kingdom, and a high wall separated it from the "elegant" side. There, in front of the living room, big square tiles of white Carrara marble extended for several meters into the garden, forming a graceful strip skirted by lusciously blooming flowerbeds. On *la terrazza*, weather-worn wicker chairs formed an inviting circle, and behind them a wrought-iron flower étagère stood against the wall. Myriad geraniums spilled from their pots: pink, red, orange, white.

A huge plumbago bush almost entirely covered the kitchen wall, its pale blue flowers looking as if drawn by a child's hand: five simple petals emerging from long, spidery stems. At the foot of the wall, more pots of multicolored geraniums and intensely perfumed herbs were set on simple wooden shelves, supported by unadorned bricks. I spent many hours strolling in and out of the kitchen where I had found my culinary calling and where my aptitude had unquestionably elevated me to a higher position in Emilia's eyes.

Unfortunately, I was not a perfect disciple, stubbornness being one of the most distinctive features of my personality. One day I spent several hours standing with my face turned to the plumbago blossoms, punishment for having treated Emilia rudely during one of our cooking sessions. *"Lo pulisci tu!* Clean it yourself!" I had answered petulantly to Emilia's order to clean up the puddle of milk I'd spilled on the kitchen floor. My mother, who had just happened to wander into the kitchen and witnessed my insolence, made me stand on the kitchen patio facing the wall without moving until I was ready to apologize.

"Come ti permetti? How could you answer back in such an unpleasant way? Remember that you owe Emilia the same respect you owe your family," Mamma admonished sternly. "You will stand here until you say you are sorry." My seven-year-old pride forbade me from apologizing too quickly, so I waited until a reasonable amount of time had expired and my status slowly turned into quasi martyrdom. I felt queasy, my legs throbbed from standing, and my eyes were tired from wandering over the plumbago bush. For a couple of hours, I counted each blossom and closely studied each petal and leaf. Holding my hands tightly crossed behind my back, I carefully scrutinized every string and thread of Emilia's scrubbing brushes and mop. I focused my attention on a tiny column of black ants courageously crossing the cats' dish to steal forgotten crumbs.

In the end, I dragged my unwilling feet in front of an embarrassed Emilia. *"Scusa,"* I mumbled, hiding consonants and vowels under my uncooperative tongue. I scowled, my eyes fixed on the gray tiles, my face barely visible under the wisps of hair escaping from my tightly pulled braids.

My mother did not like what she witnessed and, taking me firmly by one arm, said in her calmly threatening way, "Either you feel what you are saying, or else."

I ran sobbing into Emilia's arms and all was forgiven.

In the kitchen we had a late-nineteenth-century stove made of white enamel and iron. It came with big concentric rings that could be removed or added to accommodate different-sized pots and pans. The fewer rings, the more heat: the flames flared up, flickering under the larger pots, licking their sides and leaving behind long dark stains. A rectangular copper cauldron filled with water boiled steadily for the continuous needs of the house. A solitary ladle emerged from the bubbling water, its handle bobbing in unison with the rhythm of the heat waves, ready to fill a pot of tea or add liquid to a *risotto*.

This stove required constant stoking with coal. Emilia trotted up and down the steep stairway that led to the coal room, situated directly under the kitchen in the basement. The most forbidding room in the house and the quintessence of darkness, the coal room featured a small window that allowed only traces of spooky light to filter in. Intrepid Emilia carried up the coal to stoke the fire, managing to keep the heat at a controlled temperature, ready to raise it when needed.

Big white cupboards, decorated with carved fruits and leaves, stood along the south wall of the kitchen, holding simple everyday utensils and humble plates and vases. The big pots, mementos of the better times before World War II, when the family had entertained lavishly, lay abandoned in a cluster on the bottom shelves except for the three occasions a year—Christmas, New Year's, and Easter—when they finally came alive.

A rectangular wooden table with a white marble top stood in the center of the room, in front of the stove. A substantial number of wooden spoons resided in its drawer, carefully categorized according to which foods they were supposed to stir, whip, or fold. *"Non confondere i mestoli!* Make sure you never mix up the spoons!" A strict de facto segregation reigned in the formal meritocracy of Emilia's spoons, and I had to learn its rules, dictated by the food being cooked. The long-handled spoons destined solely for pasta and needed to reach the secluded recesses of the huge pots occupied the left side of the drawer.

"Wood absorbs the flavors, *sta attenta!*" Emilia cautioned. Flavors could not be muddled; this would alter the taste.

My favorite spoon was the small crooked one that for decades had been used for chocolate, to stir the rich *mousse au chocolat,* or the *budino di cioccolato e pere,* the chocolate and pear pudding I loved so much. Its sides were bent and worn by the many years of immersion in melting chocolate. There was a missing piece, a notch that gave the spoon the look of a five-year-old whose smile is missing a tooth. I could recognize it among all its companions with my eyes shut, simply by feeling its uneven edge with my fingers.

❦ Budino di Cioccolato e Pere ❦
CHOCOLATE AND PEAR PUDDING

This is one of the dishes my brother and sisters asked Emilia to make most frequently. Good news: it is easy, and it can be prepared the day before. When the pudding is cool, refrigerate it, but bring it to room temperature before serving. For my first attempts, Emilia had me use a soufflé dish. She could serve it from the mold and I didn't risk ruining it or losing face! Keep in mind that the baking time will be slightly different depending on the mold you use (heavy or light, metal or ceramic).

For the pears
    2 ripe but firm Bosc pears
    3 tablespoons sugar
    Juice of 2 lemons
    ½ teaspoon ground cinnamon

Peel, halve, and core the pears. Put them in a saucepan with the sugar, lemon juice, and cinnamon, add water to cover, and bring to a boil. Lower the heat and simmer for about 20 minutes, or until the pears are tender when pierced with a knife. Use a slotted spoon to transfer the pears to a plate to cool, then cut into bite-sized pieces.

For the pudding
    3⅔ cups milk
    4 ounces bittersweet chocolate
    4 ounces (about 20) Amaretti di Saronno cookies
        (available in Italian and other specialty stores),
        crushed
    4 ounces (about 12) savoiardi cookies or ladyfingers,
        crushed
    ¼ cup sugar
    3 large eggs
    5 tablespoons finely ground almonds
    ½ teaspoon ground cinnamon

Bring the milk to a boil in a medium saucepan. Finely chop the chocolate, and put it into a bowl. Pour about ⅔ cup of the hot milk over the chocolate, and whisk until smooth. Add the chocolate mixture to the saucepan, along with the amaretti, savoiardi, and sugar. Whisk over low heat for 10 minutes, or until smooth. Transfer to a bowl and set aside to cool to room temperature.

Preheat the oven to 350°F. Butter a 9-inch Bundt pan, and dust with sugar, tapping out the excess. Fill a roasting pan with 2 inches of hot water.

When the chocolate mixture is cool, whisk in the eggs one by one, followed by the almonds, cinnamon, and diced pears. Pour the mixture into the mold. Put the mold into the roasting pan and carefully transfer to the oven. Loosely cover the mold with aluminum foil, and bake for 1 hour and 15 minutes.

Remove the foil, increase the oven temperature to 400°F, and bake for 10 minutes more. Tap the pan lightly; the pudding should be set but still a bit wobbly. Remove from the oven, and let cool to room temperature.

Makes 6 servings

Emilia was graced with a pair of steel hands; scorching-hot pots and pans never affected them. Under my incredulous eyes, she lifted lids, inspected food, and tasted piping-hot sauces without using the crocheted pot holders Mamma and Nonna industriously produced. She persistently snubbed those unshapely multicolored remnants of former favorite sweaters that hung from the wall. *"Vedrai, Bimba, è una questione di tempo,"* she asserted, offering hope that time and experience would likewise transform my hands into calloused instruments impervious to heat and flames.

The huge black cast-iron pots Emilia maneuvered with such dexterity—on the rare occasions she was allowed to prepare fried dishes—had to be meticulously oiled after each use. For this task, she used a special saffron-orange paper, the kind with which butchers and fishmongers wrapped food. She carefully unfolded the fillet of fish or the pound of ground meat as soon as she returned from the market, smoothing wrinkles, pressing borders, and straightening the big square pieces of paper, accumulating them day after day in tidy heaps on one of the shelves of the pantry armoire. The moment she finished using a pot, Emilia took a piece and wiped away the grease with a circular movement of her hand.

Not a drop of dish soap was allowed to interfere in the cleansing of those pots. *"Il sapone distrugge il ferro,"* Emilia scornfully claimed; it was a well-accepted domestic axiom that any trace of soap would quickly ruin the iron. Emilia continued to swab the sides and the bottom of the pot until it was clean, retaining a faint shine, still resplendent with the oil's luster. Only then did she carefully pile it atop the other pots inside the big armoire.

"Pulisci mentre cucini!" Emilia counseled. Cleaning up as you cooked was an imperative: a real cook had to learn to keep the kitchen spotlessly clean and tidy, especially during the preparation of an elaborate meal.

Triglie al Tegame alla Livornese
PANFRIED MULLET

1 medium onion
1 clove garlic
½ cup packed flat-leaf parsley leaves

¼ cup extra-virgin olive oil

6 whole mullet (each about 7 ounces), scaled and gutted

Salt and freshly ground pepper *a piacere*

3 tablespoons flour

½ cup Emilia's Tomato Sauce (page 5)

½ bay leaf

Peel and mince the onion and garlic. Finely chop the parsley, and combine with the onion and garlic.

Warm the olive oil in a heavy frying pan, preferably cast-iron, over medium heat. Pat the mullet dry with a paper towel. Season with salt and pepper, and dust lightly with the flour. When the oil is hot, put the mullet in the pan and cook for 3 minutes. Turn them delicately, and cover with the parsley mixture. Pour in the tomato sauce, add the bay leaf, and cook for about 3 minutes more, until the fish flakes easily when poked with a fork. Discard the bay leaf before serving.

When you are finished, remember to clean the pan!

Makes 6 servings

One day, when I was eight, Emilia announced that she would take me to Vada, the small village on the sea a few kilometers from Livorno where her entire family lived. My mother granted permission, and off we went. Taking *la corriera*, the old blue bus that carried all sorts of people and merchandise from town to town, was part of the wonderful adventure.

"*Vestiti elegante*," she made sure to instruct me. Naturally, I had to dress up; Emilia wouldn't have it otherwise. It was a question of "face": certainly I would have lowered her social status in the eyes of her neighbors had I appeared in my everyday clothes. Consequently, I put on my elegant yellow dress with the smocked front. My mother pulled my hair into the usual tight braids; I wore my brown sandals, and held Emilia's hand in great anticipation. "*Allora? Quando arriviamo?* How long before we get there?" I skipped and bounced, tugging at her brown sweater sleeve.

Vada exerted a powerful attraction. I knew that at Emilia's home I would be the center of attention. It seemed like a great idea for a short respite from my everyday life where my brother, Paolo, and my newborn sister, Giovanna, crowded the via Roma house, competing for attention, taking away from my important status of eldest child.

The *corriera* took us slowly to Vada, stopping at every town and village along the way, finally delivering us outside the tiny station in the middle of the village. From there a broad avenue, flanked by centuries-old plane trees, took us directly to the beach. Humble one-story houses opened up in an orderly line along the sea. They all looked alike: red tile roofs, faded ocher walls that had seen better days, and tiny pieces of land, optimistically called *i giardinetti,* the small gardens in front. Rosemary, basil, zinnias, and roses lived together, sharing a crowded space, resilient in the salty winter winds, impervious to the summer heat waves. Superb white calla lilies adorned the front doors, recipients of vigorous downpours of dishwater after the end of every meal. Italian housewives have always been convinced that this treatment is precisely what these plants wish for: they, in fact, seem to respond exuberantly, thriving under soapy blitzkriegs.

I sat and ate with Emilia's sister Ada, her two brothers, and sisters-in-law; they were a family of fishermen, and the food on the table surpassed even my wildest dreams. Emilia and the women of the family served us *cacciucco,* a thick fish soup with morsels of every conceivable marine creature, generously ladled over great slices of bread rubbed with garlic. We devoured *pasta al pomodoro,* with red pepper flakes and *basilico,* and *triglie al tegame,* the crimson skin of the mullet competing in redness with the garlicky tomato sauce. Why couldn't my grandparents understand the superiority of Emilia's taste? Why on earth did they want to stick to their bland food?

We ate perfect Tuscan sweet peas, tender green beans, and young spinach quickly sautéed in olive oil, while Emilia poked her little finger into the trays to single out the best bits of food for me, whispering, *"Prendi questo!* Take this!" To my grandmother, this "pinky-poking" represented the single most infuriating aspect of Emilia's behavior. But Emilia just couldn't refrain from it, especially when she thought that "her" children could benefit from her knowledgeable choice of the most tender morsel of veal or the perfect piece of cheese. At our table, it amused me to see a cloud of unhappiness shrouding Nonna's face as soon as Emilia perpetrated this ill-mannered action. No warnings or lectures ever stopped her.

Pisellini di Vada
SWEET PEAS WITH HAM

Emilia, of course, used only fresh peas. After returning from the market, we sat around the kitchen table or out in the garden, shelling *pisellini,* sweet peas. Separating the tiny peas from their pods was a delicious exercise: handfuls always had a way of ending up in my mouth rather than in the white enamel bowl.

2 pounds peas in the pod, shelled, or one 10-ounce
    package frozen fancy petite peas, thawed
1 medium onion, peeled and finely chopped
½ cup finely chopped ham, prosciutto, or bacon
4 tablespoons unsalted butter
1 tablespoon extra-virgin olive oil
1 teaspoon sugar
⅓ cup chicken broth
⅓ cup dry white wine
Salt and freshly ground pepper *a piacere*

Sauté the peas, onion, and ham in the butter and olive oil in
a large saucepan over medium heat, stirring, until the onion
begins to soften, about 5 minutes. Add the sugar. Pour in the
chicken broth and white wine, season with salt and pepper,
and simmer until the peas are tender and most of the liquid
has evaporated, about 10 minutes.

Makes 6 servings

After lunch, Emilia and her family took me to the beach. "Do you
want to see the hut where my brothers keep all the fish and lobsters?" she suggested with an anticipatory smile. The prospect of
a walk to the immense beach that ran for kilometers, empty
except for a few fishermen's shacks, was greatly alluring. The
seemingly endless flat vistas were interrupted only by the tower-
ing chimney stacks of Stabilimento Solvay, the mammoth Belgian
factory that produced sodium carbonate. A perpetual plume of
silvery smoke rose high from the funnels, drawing fantastic

arabesques that evaporated imperceptibly in the afternoon sky. The strip of sea immediately in front of the factory appeared an extraordinary shade of chalky white, due to the residues of soda continuously spewed into the Tyrrhenian waters.

Down we went, that Sunday afternoon, to the gray hut. Nets and buoys, old rags, and battered olive cans were stacked in front of the door. Emilia's family's venerable rowboat was tightly secured to a large cement block with several ropes, and the few wooden planks used to drag it from the sea lay neatly at its side. It was a wonderful afternoon, serene and calm, the waves now relaxed into a gentle washing against the sandy shore. One of Emilia's brothers sat on the sand, patiently preparing the nets for the evening. He gently unfolded them inch by inch, cleaning them, extracting clots of dry seaweed and twigs stuck inside the holes, leftover from the early morning catch. His eyes focused on the task, removing old barnacles and efficiently repairing the tears caused by the strong Mediterranean tuna and the frantically gyrating squid. *"Guarda!"* He nodded toward the black ink stains that blotched sections of the net; the squid must have been desperate to free themselves. He worked methodically, without wasted movements, the experience of a lifetime reflected in his efficient handling of the bulky nets. He accumulated the cork-ball floats—their original color faded by the intense sun—on one side of the boat and folded the mesh in tidy, regular layers on the other. As I looked on, absorbed by the uniform repetition of his work, the afternoon breeze sprayed a salty mist of sea and sand on my face. The fishing equipment emanated its distinctively acrid smell of old ropes, decaying marine life, and desiccated shells.

The other brother, a short olive-skinned man, squatted at the water's edge, rhythmically hurling a big gray octopus against one of the rocks. *Wham! Slam! Bam!* He took his prey by the tentacles and bashed it ten, twenty times against the hard surface. "*Vedi?* We must soften it, otherwise it isn't good to eat," Emilia explained, noticing my surprise. "The octopus flesh can be very hard and inedible; it is important to tenderize it correctly before cooking," she continued. Her brother put his hand inside the octopus and turned it inside out like an old sock. The poor beast sprawled on the sand, a light gray heap of limp arms and deflated pink suckers. He grabbed it and started to scrape it against the rock exactly the way I had seen Emilia wash the collars of my grandfather's shirts. A whitish, slimy foam began exuding from the octopus, dribbling down the rock, shining under the sun's rays. I had never seen anything like this, and stored the information inside, savoring the moment I would disclose it to my brother, Paolo. Life with Emilia was indeed full of surprises.

"*Fatto!* The octopus is ready!" Emilia's brother announced. Emilia picked it up and placed it in a basket, ready to transport it to Livorno to make a good *cacciucco* for us.

"Have you ever seen live lobsters?" one of the brothers asked me, gently pushing me inside the open door to admire the catch of the day. What seemed like hundreds—better thousands—of huge, beet-red lobsters clamored and clumped, thundered and banged, clattered and bawled, crawling toward me. I screamed with all the force of my lungs and ran into Emilia's arms. Her brothers, amused by my shock, collapsed on the white sand, laughing goodnaturedly at the sight of the little city girl terrorized by a few defenseless crustaceans.

Late in the afternoon, Emilia filled her bulky black bag with all kinds of fish and vegetables, carefully topping it with ricotta made from sheep's milk, fresh figs, and the octopus whose untimely end I had witnessed. It was time to go back to Livorno, and Ada, Emilia's sister, would take the *corriera* with us.

Ada was casually and affectionately referred to, by her own loving sister, as *la mi'Ada strabica* (my squint-eyed Ada). In fact, it seemed impossible to look straight into her eyes, as they had a very unsettling way of wandering elsewhere even while she concentrated on us. My brother and sisters and I loved her very much. Smaller than Emilia, and round as a doughnut, she frequently came to spend the night at our house. She wore her hair in a tight bun, with big brown pins that often escaped from the knot.

"Dai, Ada! Ti posso pettinare?" I loved being allowed to loosen and comb her chestnut tresses. I would step on a chair to reach her head and, with great satisfaction, stick those pins inside her mane to better support her elaborate coiffure. Mamma didn't really approve of my early passion for hairdressing and outlawed what she deemed an unseemly activity. I naturally thought otherwise and made sure to escape her surveillance, plunging my willing hands into Ada's abundant hair as often as possible.

Ada was Emilia's useful alter ego; no matter what was said or done in our home, Emilia always declared that her sister knew better. If, for example, my grandmother had instructed Emilia to prepare a Chantilly cream for dessert, Emilia would answer that *"la mi'Ada strabica* thinks we should prepare a *zabaione."* It was a fight between titans, my gentle but firm grandmother and Emilia's almost invincible surrogate. Sometimes Nonna decided to let herself be beaten at the game and exhaustedly lifted her hands in the air proclaiming: *"Va bene, va bene . . ."*

Emilia was very stubborn. When I was eight, my mother received a washing machine, an extravagant Christmas gift from our famous uncle Corrado, the richest person in our family. The bulky contrivance, built of heavy wood and metal, was placed prominently in the big bathroom on the third floor. A wooden roller connected to a big crank that looked like a huge flexed arm protruded awkwardly from the machine; its purpose was to squeeze water from the linen. Paolo and I loved to feed the ominous-looking roller with dripping sheets, one of us in charge of the crank, the other receiving the cloth emerging from the other side. "*Attento, Paolo!* Here it comes!" We were mesmerized by seeing those voluminous bedsheets reduced to flat pancakes.

"*È un'invenzione del diavolo.* It's an invention of the devil," Emilia proclaimed. I can still see her drying her hands on the big apron wrapped tightly around her stocky little body, shaking her head with disdain at the idea of this intrusion into her well-ordered life. "*Il Buon Dio* has given us a pair of hands," she grumbled. What was, *nel nome di Dio,* a fabrication like that doing in a proper house like ours? Surely it had been invented to steal jobs from the pitiable wage earners like herself. She refused to use the machine.

Sparkling brass was one of Emilia's great prides. It had to glimmer and shine. Brass and silver were treated with the same unremitting respect. Their care added to the daily work load, but their luster affirmed the household's elegance and therefore the superiority and indispensability of its sovereign: our beloved Emilia. The Italian phrase *sugo di gomito* (elbow grease) aptly describes the high-energy, high-endurance scrubbing and scouring that regularly went on at our doorstep. The most activity was lavished upon the big knobs that decorated the massive walnut front door. Emilia seemed convinced that her social status and the subsequent respect she gained were directly related to the luster of these knobs. Arriving home at midday, when our school day was over, we would find her outside the door, stretching on her tiptoes to reach her target, armed with pieces of old cloth and the bottle of Sidol, the smelly cleaning liquid.

We children were absolutely forbidden to touch the brass; if we dared, we would suffer Emilia's wrath. Unfortunately, the adults had to use an enormous black iron key to open the door and in so doing had to give the knobs a vigorous yank, leaving behind a trail of fingerprints. *"Dio bonino! Madonnina mia,"* Emilia would say with a sigh, asking God and the omnipresent Virgin Mary to help her. It was not her position to complain, but she made her unhappiness very clear to anyone who saw her lips tighten into a thin line. She rolled her eyes to the sky, imploring *Gesummaria e tutti i Santi* (Jesus, Mary, and all the saints) to provide her with great patience. Emilia herself had no reason to touch the knobs, since she used the service entrance. *"È tutta colpa loro,"* she often muttered. It was solely my family's fault if the fingerprints ravaged the elegant entrance to our house.

Emilia went out every morning in her brown tweed coat, clutching her *borsa della spesa,* the big net bag that would contain all the treasures from the *mercato coperto,* the old covered market. Sometimes during school holidays, if I were really lucky, I would get to go too. Everybody knew Emilia, and that meant lots of face time for me. The *macellaio* would lean over the marble counter— amid bloody quarters of beef, filet mignon, pork trotters and ribs—and notice how much I had grown. *"Signorinella!* Didn't you just turn seven? You seem to grow like an asparagus!" The *salumiere* would wink and slice a wedge of pecorino cheese and a thick chunk of local prosciutto for me to taste. Fresh ricotta glistened behind the glass case, the tantalizing promise of a *merenda* to come. Ricotta, sugar, and cocoa powder—what better snack could one wish for?

Stepping inside the beautiful fin de siècle brick and wrought-iron *mercato* was like entering another world. An immense sky-light filtered the sunshine and enveloped the enormous hall in a greenish hue. Light flooded over the booths, highlighting the heaps of vegetables, creeping through the individual planks of the stands, and shimmering in the puddles of water that sat underneath the stalls. The voices of shoppers and vendors raised and lowered in a comfortably unintelligible clamor, joining together into what seemed like an incantation. *"Donne, comprate!* Come, women! Buy from me! *Le belle melanzane!* The best egg-plants! They are almost for free!" intoned the merchants. "I am going bankrupt for you women. Buy! They are practically a gift." Emilia never listened. She looked and touched and smelled, test-ing tomatoes, checking the firmness of the zucchini, anticipating their taste.

"You call this a gift? I would never pay these prices. . . ." she would proclaim, scorning the beautiful purple *melanzane*. She loved playing the oldest game of all, sneering at the greengrocer and demeaning his offerings in the hopes of extracting a lower price.

Emilia's market techniques, honed by the war years and the need for survival, represented a formidable compendium of skill and astuteness, combined with an incredible *faccia tosta*, a cheeky attitude that delivered rewarding results. In order to be proficient at the daily market skirmishes, there were some basic rules—or lack of same—one had to keep in mind. Rule One was that there is no such thing as a line. Why waste time and miss a valuable opportunity to snatch the best piece of meat or the freshest fish? Two was never to make eye contact with the com-petitor. Perceiving the person in front of you as a human being was dangerous; age, sex, and frailty would come into the picture and weaken your resolution to win. Three was to position your frame in such a way that your elbows protected your space and propelled you efficiently toward the produce. Four was to exploit the well-known love and consideration Italians lavish on children. *"Attenzione alla bimba!"* screamed Emilia, her extended elbows providing me a refuge from her adversaries. A fraction of a second, and our neighbor—obviously not versed in Rules Two and Four—was defeated. I had been recognized as a child and Emilia had successfully inched toward the sweetest melons.

I discovered that many interesting things went on under the booths. Cats of every shape and color stretched and licked themselves, lazily watching for mice. I played with the discarded vegetables on the ground, pushing a fennel core with the tip of my foot toward the little black dog that sat patiently behind the greengrocer's stand. Would the eager mutt eat it? *"Bimba!* Not with those good shoes, what will your mother say?" Emilia tugged me away.

Behind the stands sat the greengrocers' wives, trimming vegetables for their clients. They peeled and diced carrots and potatoes, split chubby artichokes, discarded spinach stems—pulling off any tough fibers—slit parsnips, and eventually dropped all into galvanized steel buckets filled with water. During the winter months, it was black cabbage, broccoli of all kinds and colors, lush white fennel, and the many vegetables needed for the perfect minestrone. In June, I loved to watch the women shelling fresh *fagioli rossi* (red beans), separating the pods and sending the variegated pink and white beans into the container of water, where they would bob and float and finally rest on the bottom as if weariness had suddenly overcome them. "Imagine paying a premium to have them shelled!" Emilia exclaimed with renewed scorn each summer.

Fish stands and butcher shops lined the perimeter of the huge building, sending my senses into overdrive—and not always in a positive way. Emilia would place her meat order and the particular cut was sliced, cleaned, and packaged in saffron-colored parchment paper—all as we watched. Entire carcasses hung from thick iron hooks. The butchers, wrapped in bloodstained white aprons, thought nothing of using their big knives to quarter the animal in front of the shoppers, blood dripping on the sawdust spread on the floor to minimize the mess. The postslaughter sweeping fascinated me most. At the end of her husband's grim activity, the butcher's wife would emerge from behind the counter, armed with broom and pail. Within seconds, she had collected the liquid and the various droppings that had coagulated in the sawdust. No rags, no water, no mopping.

The fishmongers' was the worst, not just because of the smell. I hated to walk by the barrels that sat outside the walls of the shops, brimming with desiccated codfish buried under tons of salt. Sooty gray, the fish looked to me like goatskins that had spent months under the sun. I knew the codfish was a staple of our horrible Catholic meatless Fridays and that sooner or later Emilia would have to stock it. I always tried to avoid those containers, whose stench was enough to make me retch. *"Emilia, andiamo.* Let's go home. Please!"

"Girellini un soldo l'uno, bimbi piangete che mamma ve li 'ompra!" intoned the old man at the market. "Go on, children, cry! If you do, your mother will then buy you my pinwheels!" He obviously needed no marketing tips. I yearned for everything he sold: colorful balloons, elaborately striped pastel candies, sugar sticks, and *girellini.* But with Emilia exercising her usual restraint, I always ended up settling for a *frate,* the best treat on my marketing days, a very light doughnut sold at Adriano's. Literally a hole in the wall in one in the dilapidated, crumbling

buildings in the Piazza del Mercato, the shop was just big enough for Adriano and his huge cauldron of boiling oil. He made and sold the best *frati*. Under my fascinated stare, he would plop the ring-shaped piece of dough into the bubbling oil and *hop!* it would reemerge after a few seconds, cooked to golden perfection. After fishing it out, he would roll the *frate* quickly in sugar, then, with a deft movement, wrap it in brown paper and hand it to me, a most delighted customer.

"I frati! I frati! Venite gente!" Adriano shouted to the mass of potential customers that hurried along in front of his store. People came from everywhere to eat *i frati di Adriano,* and they sang his praises all over Tuscany.

LA MIA FAMIGLIA TOSCANA

Back row, from left: *Zio Marcello, Zia Marilena,*
Zio Pierluigi, Papà, the author, and Nonno;
front row: *Nonna, Mamma, and Paolo*

My grandmother's everyday dining room table was meticulously white. The plates matched the white napkins to their left; the crystal glasses seemed to sparkle white; and even the ivory handles of the silver knives blended in with the blanched, colorless world around them. And, of course, the food that graced the table was also white.

Seasonal flowers—freesias, dahlias, and roses—simply arranged in short silver vases added the only color to the room. For the cyclamen plants, crowded at the foot of the two tall windows that opened from the dining room onto the via Roma side of the house, the prevailing hue was again white, in all its ever-changing shades. The delicate ivory flowers clustered abundantly under the shade of the oval leaves, arching and curving their willowy stems; their stylish five-petal crowns gracefully emerged from the mass of dark green foliage.

The oval mahogany table was always kept ready, the table-cloths reaching halfway to the floor. The white-on-white damask tablecloths had been woven especially for the family, with scenes of hunting or fishing or various floral subjects. "Your great-grandfather Luigi ordered them in Belgium, in the famous Flanders workshops," my mother told me with admiration and pride.

The silver napkin rings that indicated the occupant of each place were among the most engaging items at the table. The individual names, engraved in an elaborate antique style, established the dining room hierarchy: Nonno GianPaolo and Nonna Valentina at the ends of the table, my parents, Luciana and Adolfo (when he wasn't away sailing with the navy), at their sides. My mother's brothers, Zio Marcello and Zio Pierluigi, who sometimes joined the family on Sundays with their respective wives, Zia Marilena and Zia Laura, sat in between.

Decorated with intricate initials and dates, the napkin rings had been manufactured by famous and skillful silversmiths on the occasions of celebratory anniversaries: weddings, important birthdays, first communions. My father and mother used those inherited from my father's family, the Grills. They seemed to sparkle much less than those of my mother's family, the Langs, but in my eyes, they were infinitely more beautiful; fabulous silver dragons, almost hidden under a profusion of allegorical leaves and flowers, crawled and twisted around each one. I spent hours contemplating these examples of mythological elegance and beauty. My fingers traced the shapes of the ferocious beasts whose fierce heads, adorned by long horns, faced each other in shows of cruel savagery. A fat sun, with its conventional bursting rays, beamed between the two dragons. I closed my eyes and shivered, exploring their dangerous spikes.

The combination of Nonno's diabetes and his pleasure in observing a precise schedule translated into rigidly established lunch and dinner hours. Lunch was served at half past noon, marking the end of our school day and his midday break from the office. Dinnertime was strictly set at 7:30. At lunch, considered the most important meal of the day, Emilia served her heaviest dishes. Engulfed in a white apron, almost lost in its starched expanse, she moved around the table, not so silently offering her trays of delicacies and busily intent on making sure that "her" family was well fed. Pasta and rice were the protagonists of the midday meal, and they came in many guises: *lasagne al forno, maccheroncini prosciutto e bechamelle,* and the little *nidi di capellini,* whimsical nests of capellini filled with minutely diced veal and baked in the oven. The range of *risotti* made good use of seasonal vegetables like artichokes, asparagus, and sweet peas. More often than not, though, there was a collegial request for *pasta in bianco,* a simple dish of spaghetti, butter, and Parmesan cheese. Red meat was seldom served, fish, chicken, spinach, or chicory being preferred.

My grandparents were addicted to a marvelous product, L'Idrolitina del Cavalier Gazzoni, the economical postwar way of creating instantaneous sparkling water at a time when it still represented an extravagant expense. It was as simple as counting to three, a packetful of a mysterious powder the only element needed. Perfectly calculated for a liter of water, the contents were dropped inside a bottle, immediately producing an extraordinary quantity of bubbles. Who needed to spend money buying the local *acqua minerale Corallo* that sprang from a source near Livorno Station?

"*Allora?* May I help? What can I do?" I pressed Emilia zealously. My eagerly awaited duty was to execute the alchemy that transformed tap water into a fancy drink. I climbed onto a chair and carefully tore open the packet of Idrolitina, pouring its contents into the special glass bottles my grandparents kept for their "*acqua minerale.*"

Watching the carbon dioxide mix in the water was almost as satisfactory as The Dropping of the Saccharine. My brother, Paolo, and I anxiously awaited the end of every meal and a motion from Nonno's white head inviting us to run to his side to admire the tiny pills being dropped into hot black coffee. His long fingers extracted the plastic container from his pocket. The pill that plunged into the scorching beverage produced a bomb-like effect of foam, while myriad concentric white rings unfurled on the surface, unleashing whimsical patterns. Another triumph of home chemistry.

The after-lunch siesta was imperative. Nonno retired into his office and discreetly closed the doors behind him. When he was home, Papà dropped into his favorite armchair, closed his eyes, and fell asleep at once. "Being an officer helps," he explained. Papà could sleep and wake up on command; nothing would disturb him, not even the noise of his children playing next to him. This useful skill had been acquired on board ship, where duty would call him on deck at unexpected hours. Mamma and Nonna looked forward to relaxing, reading *Il Tirreno,* the local newspaper, and studying the precious trove of knitting and embroidering instructions found in their favorite magazines.

"Food is better digested at lunchtime because the afternoon activities provide for an optimal assimilation of calories and proteins," Mamma would explain after lunch, contradicting herself within minutes. *"A nanna!"* she declared, using the babyish noun that defined the torturous couple of hours Paolo and I had to spend in our beds in the middle of the day. Whatever happened to those afternoon plans my mother had spoken about? It was maddening; Paolo and I were dragged to our afternoon nap and the house became terribly quiet.

On Sundays, the eleven o'clock Mass at Santa Giulia ruled the life of the via Roma household. A specific series of tasks had to be completed by the time we all set out the door at 10:30. Immediately after breakfast, Nonno set all the clocks in the house. He moved methodically and unhurriedly, Sunday after Sunday, repeating the same precise gestures. After opening the glass door of the imposing grandfather clock in the hall, he extracted the heavy brass key and inserted it in the slot exactly in the middle of the dial plate, turning it several times to wind the mechanism. His surprisingly nimble big fingers moved the minute hand forward, setting the right time. Satisfied with his work, he stepped back to admire the results, happy to have improved the harmony of the household. "Punctuality is the characteristic of kings," he would lecture me. "Remember: to be late is insulting for those who are waiting for you." He then continued his systematic mission, walking through the tall glass doors into the pantry, where he checked the plate-shaped clock with the white china front. To plan the family's stringent meal hours, Emilia always needed to be aware of the time, and Nonno happily contributed to the cause. Upstairs he repeated the same motions in the library and the bedroom, setting the time in all the different timepieces that adorned the bookshelves, the chest of drawers, and Nonna's desk. Then the new week was finally allowed to commence, on time.

The task of grinding coffee beans in the exact quantity needed for the entire week ahead was assigned to Paolo and me. We sat at the kitchen table and proudly released the little hatch in the brass hinge of the grinder, unbolting it to feed the beans into the green tin machine. Around and around we cranked the wooden handle of the old *macinacaffè*. The rhythm was hypnotic and the sensual smell of the freshly ground coffee inebriated us.

"*Patrizia, che ne pensi?* Do you think it is enough?" asked Paolo anxiously, measuring the coffee that nearly overflowed the drawer.

"*Basta, basta!* Enough!" my mother exclaimed, arriving just in time to avert a disastrous spilling of the costly black powder.

Since Emilia had Sunday afternoons off, Mamma prepared her wonderful Sunday specialty: *gnocchi di semolino,* the delicate dish made of semolina flour. She boiled water and milk, added a substantial quantity of flour, and stirred until the mass reached a smooth, quasi-solid consistency. With a touch or two of a cleverly handled spoon, she spread the golden expanse on the marble tabletop. A pat here, a pat there, and the mixture was then cut into perfectly round disks. Layered in an ovenproof serving dish and generously sprinkled with Parmesan cheese and butter, this marvel of simple home cooking was ready to be baked. Emilia made sure to put it in the oven at precisely a quarter to twelve; when Nonno came back from church, lunch had to be ready—no excuses allowed.

✣ *Gnocchi di Semolino di Mamma* ✣
MAMMA'S GNOCCHI

For the dough
    1 quart milk
    1 cup water
    Salt *a piacere*
    1 cup semolina flour
    1 cup freshly grated Parmesan cheese
    2 large eggs
    4 tablespoons unsalted butter
    1 tablespoon olive oil

Bring the milk and water to a boil in a large saucepan. Salt the liquid. Slowly add the flour, a little at a time, whisking constantly to avoid lumps. Remove from the heat and, with a wooden spoon, mix in the Parmesan cheese. Quickly stir in the eggs and butter. Spread a thin film of olive oil on a clean counter and pour out the mixture, spreading it evenly with a wooden spoon or spatula until it is about ½-inch thick. Press a piece of plastic wrap directly against the surface of the dough. Let cool to room temperature.

To bake
    ½ cup freshly grated Parmesan cheese
    3 tablespoons unsalted butter

Preheat the oven to 375°F.

Cut the dough into ⅔-inch rounds with a cookie cutter and arrange them—overlapping, like fallen dominoes—in a

12-inch ovenproof serving dish. Sprinkle the top with the Parmesan cheese and dot with the butter. Bake for 20 minutes, or until golden brown, then cover loosely with foil and continue baking for 15 minutes.

Raise the oven temperature to 400°F and bake for a final 10 minutes until cooked through.

Makes 6 servings

Religion played an important role in our family life. Holidays and sacred festivities were rigorously observed. On Sundays and *le feste comandate* (Holy Days of Obligation) our family attended the solemn Mass at Santa Giulia, a tiny seventeenth-century chapel in the old part of the city. It was dark and elegant, with an ancient, heavily inlaid wooden choir.

A hard-earned proficiency in finding distractions allowed me to ignore the never-ending sermons. The choir, always filled to capacity with men dressed in spooky white vestments, served as a perfect resource. I studied their creepy hoods and the wooden crosses that hung on their chests and mulled over their reasons for being dressed in such a weird, scary way. I pondered the incongruity of the elegant black lace-up shoes that emerged from beneath their medieval white garb. Their white hoods only half-hid their features, still revealing big Tuscan noses, prominently silhouetted against the darkness of the church. Members of La Confraternita della Misericordia, one of many traditions leftover from feudal times, these men dedicated their lives to good deeds and endless religious processions and rites.

As soon as I could read, I discovered that the Gospels were an absorbing and fascinating element of Sunday rites. Avidly searching through my missal, I jumped from celebration to celebration, canvasing every month of the year for a good story. During a January Mass, I would discreetly devour the March and April readings. By September, I had already pored over the November and December passages, ignoring the words the priest solemnly uttered from the altar. Unlike Jacob, I would never give up my rights as eldest for a simple plate of lentils, not even Emilia's, I told myself, puzzled by his decision. Treating the missal like an adventure book, I was never disappointed.

Sometimes my attention focused on the beautiful liturgy and elegant vestments. Even in restrained Santa Giulia, gold ran through every garment and object on and around the altar. I especially loved the incense, generously dispersed over the congregation. I approved of the priest's hieratically slow movements and appreciated the puffy clouds of spicy, musky vapor that escaped from the precious silver baskets, energetically swung by overzealous altar boys. That mist symbolized the true essence of religion, a perceivable manifestation of the all-embracing divinity.

Church chanting was intriguingly beautiful and *"Tantum Ergum Sacramentum,"* solemnly sung at the Elevation, was my favorite hymn. I belted out the enigmatic Latin words, understanding none but happy to join in the choir of elderly Livornesi. Our local accent metamorphosed each sound and amalgamated nouns and verbs. *"TantumergosaHramento"* lost quite a bit of its sacredness but certainly made the Hymn Hit Parade among Santa Giulia's devoted parishioners.

Sunday would never have been Sunday without my sauntering out of Santa Giulia at the end of the service, holding Nonno's big hand and going directly to the famous Pasticceria Pacini to buy *le mentine* and *le paste*. The first were sugar candies, tiny disks of pure pleasure that came in many colors and flavors. My favorites were the white ones with their strong mint taste, ready to melt in my mouth. *Le mentine* were Grandfather's exclusive realm. He distributed them with parsimony and only when we behaved. For Paolo and me, *le mentine* were the weekly equivalent of the Distinguished Service Cross; we received them for good services rendered.

The typical Italian treats of *le paste,* individual sweets with cream, chocolate, fruit, and sometimes liqueur, were bought and devoured all across the peninsula. In the fifties, the *pasticcerie* were (and in small provincial towns sometimes still are) the only stores allowed by the strict Italian commercial laws to open on Sunday and holiday mornings. Catering to the gastronomic pleasures of families was a duty that transcended religious and sociological beliefs.

With meticulous care, *la signora* Pacini aligned *le paste* on a silver cardboard tray. *Zabaione* and chocolate cream gushed from beignets and éclairs. She wrapped the tray, tied it tight with a golden ribbon and cleverly created a loophole for my small fingers, to help me carry home that precious parcel of sweetness.

"Ecco, Bimba, e buon appetito!" she would gently dismiss me.

Once home, my grandfather took off his Borsalino hat and hung it on the coatrack, then slid his silver-topped cane into the tall umbrella holder, an ornate ceramic urn that held his collection of antique walking sticks. Nonna, Mamma, and I went to our bedrooms to put away our missals and the antique lace veils that covered our heads in church. "Make sure you fold the veil in its pleats, and wrap it with tissue paper," my mother would admonish. "It is precious." Proud to wear it, I tried my best to be, for once, careful and tidy with this beautiful square of ivory lace that had belonged first to Nonna's mother, then Nonna, and then to Mamma when she was a child. "Later, when you turn fifteen, you will receive a black veil," my grandmother promised. A black lace veil! Could anyone dream of anything more elegant and refined? I opened my top drawer and gently put the little white bundle and the tiny missal, with its fragile mother-of-pearl cover, on the left side. I had to wait only another seven or eight years and I too would join the ranks of Ultimate Roman Catholic Sophisticates.

Traditions were hard to dodge in our household. Two ranked high on the list of possibilities for Sunday afternoons: *una girata,* a drive through the wonderful Livorno countryside, and an afternoon family *concerto.* I hated both options with all my heart. The car drive meant a boring, crowded trip, the squeezing of too many bodies inside the big Lancia, and a slow proceeding out of Livorno, up and down the surrounding hills, and twisting left and right on the tortuous dirt roads leading to Castiglioncello and Quercianella. They were Nonno's favorite places.

"Do I really have to go?" I repeatedly implored my mother to no avail. I wanted to stay home and read. Preferably on my own. Instead, I had to desert my beloved Jules Verne and Salgari, the famous Italian writer, and his Malaysian pirates, Indian thugs, and exotic princess who went by the name of Perla di Labuan.

"You know how your grandfather loves a drive," she always answered, deaf to the cries of an unwilling excursionist.

There was nothing I could do. Nonno carefully drove the big blue car out of the garage and onto via Cecconi. Displaying varying degrees of eagerness, we all climbed in: Nonno and Nonna, my mother, Paolo, Baby Giovanna, and I.

The main problem lay in Nonno's obsession with the Tuscan *paesaggio* and its ravishing beauty. Having visited the entire world, Nonno concluded that nothing compared to the Tyrrhenian coves' crystalline green water and the imposing dark rocks that framed the tiny pristine beaches. "*Bimba*, Italy is the most beautiful country in the world," he would declare.

The heavy Lancia climbed the steep hills that ran inland, parallel to the coast. Orderly lines of cypress trees seemed to dart out like fantastic feathers, following the natural contours of the slopes, rising and plunging, stretching far along the horizon. Dwarf juniper bushes, the bounteous Italian broom, all sorts of wild cytisus, and the exquisite cistus, aptly nicknamed rock rose, carpeted the harsh, windswept Livorno coast with extended yellow and white patches. In the good season, the thick Mediterranean scrub exploded with wildflowers and vigorous grasses.

The myrtle's musky scent managed to waft through the car, despite the windows always being kept tightly shut against the invasion of the all-pervading road dust. "*Chiudi subito quella finestra!* Close that window immediately!" The imperious order shouted from the front seat hit the insubordinate troops sitting in the back. What was the point in going out for *una girata* if we had to sit inside a hermetically sealed car? I asked myself, trying to lower my window imperceptibly.

Once in Quercianella or Castiglioncello, Nonno parked the car and we spilled onto the beach. I loved collecting pieces of wild red coral the waves had scattered everywhere. I filled my bucket, carefully adding the little *ombelichi della Madonna*, the sensually curved tiny white shells that reminded me of a delicately perfect navel.

Un cono alla crema was the afternoon treat that signaled the end of the pause at the beach. Then once again we had to climb into the car for the drive home.

Afternoon family concerts were equally loathsome affairs. They took place in the library on the second floor, where a big upright Bechstein sat against the wall. Two ornate bronze arms flanked the keyboard, supporting two candleholders with real candles, which occasionally, and to my great pleasure, were lit. Their flickering produced a magic game of moving shadows that made the darkening afternoons more tolerable.

Everyone sang, played, and performed. As a young man, Nonno GianPaolo, extraordinarily handsome, tall, and from a good family, had caused an uproar when he chose the drums as his musical instrument. His extravagant choice had attracted much talk in Livorno circles, and subsequent great success among the society girls. I never saw him play, but he sang well, favoring the popular tunes of the time. His voice defined him as *tenore di grazia,* or *tenorino,* as they used to say at the beginning of the century. He carried the melody gracefully and with perfect pitch. His favorite songs, regularly performed on those Sunday afternoons, were "Smoke Gets in Your Eyes" and "There Is a Little Gray Home in the West," which he and Nonna Valentina sang with stentorian voices to the applause of their unabashedly biased audience.

My grandmother was an accomplished pianist, considered by most to be extraordinarily audacious and modern in her musical taste. She loved Debussy, the revolutionary French composer, and played *Les Arabesques* with great transport.

My two uncles, who played several instruments and endlessly improvised new tunes and arrangements, experimented with jazz, classical music, and popular rhythms. Every time they convened around the piano, they launched into their signature songs: Zio Pierluigi played "Bewitched, Bothered and Bewildered" and Zio Marcello, "Tea for Two."

My brother and I considered the highlight of these evenings to be the moment when Nonna finally put her musical knowledge to good use and played the tunes we cherished, English nursery rhymes put to music. We heard of huge eggs sitting on walls before falling to certain death, of furry little creatures climbing clocks, and, my personal favorite, a curious tune about four-and-twenty blackbirds having been baked in a pie that was then offered to a king.

Among family events, Christmas was the most important of the year.

"Emilia, *facciamo la lista di Natale*," Nonna Valentina would say at the beginning of December. "What do you think we must order?"

Nonna sat at the dining room table, perusing the old notebooks of the family recipes all saved in the library on the second floor. The menu never changed much. What would a holiday be without the beloved dishes that had accompanied the various celebrations year after year over several generations? *Pasticcio di maccheroni, lasagne, arrosti.*

Preparations started several days in advance. Emilia, my mother, and my grandmother spent hours in the kitchen and pantry, and Nonna hired Concetta and Cristina to help with cooking and serving. Both women came from the surrounding countryside and were used to working under Emilia's totalitarian authority. During these major culinary missions, General Emilia led her troops to successful attack. *"Madonnina, Gesù e tuttisanti, aiutatemi,"* Emilia muttered sotto voce, charging the stove with more coal and shouting orders. I looked on from a distance, half hidden behind the glass doors that separated the kitchen from the pantry. Being a lowly member of the infantry, I was rigorously barred from the theater of operations until much later, when my skills had attained the required proficiency level.

A couple of days before Christmas, Emilia prepared the flaky, buttery *pasta frolla* (short pastry) for the *pasticcio di maccheroni,* the traditional dish that opened every celebration in the via Roma house. The pot with the thick ragù for the filling was judiciously set over the smallest rings of the stove to simmer at a low temperature for many hours. It began with finely chopped celery and carrots sautéed in olive oil and butter, and a solitary onion, sneaked in without my grandfather's knowledge. Next, leftover bits of ham, beef, veal, and finely ground pork joined the great cauldron, the meats slowly bubbling and releasing their juices. When Emilia's magic radar alerted her, she added several ladles of her famously dense tomato sauce, previously prepared and kept aside in an earthenware pot.

If I asked how long it took to simmer the meat sauce, Emilia would answer with a grumble and her usual lapidary phrase: "*Quanto basta.* As long as it takes." A pinch of salt here and there, two garlic cloves or three, one onion. It all depended on a mysterious inner voice that somehow would tell her what was needed.

Early on Christmas morning, Emilia rolled and cut the *pasta frolla* and filled it with the meat ragù, cooked *maccheroncini,* and an extra generous dose of grated Parmesan cheese. The oven put the finishing touches on the celebrated *pasticcio.* It was brought to the table once it had cooled down and the crust had absorbed the flavors of the rich sauce inside.

✿ *Pasticcio di Maccheroni* ✿
PASTA AND MEAT PIE

This recipe is probably one of the last still inspired by the culinary tradition of Imperial Rome, where sweet and savory were combined in many dishes. The contrast between the *pasticcio*'s sweet crust and its savory filling is mouthwatering and distinctive. I like to use all different kinds of meat: pork, bacon, veal, sausage, and ham. Emilia used a ratio of 6 ounces chicken livers to 10 ounces other meats. Keep in mind that, if using chicken livers, they should be cooked separately in butter and added when the other meats are ready.

Emilia's Pastry Trick: To cover the pie, roll the pastry for the top crust on wax paper or aluminum foil—of course she used a special cloth—then place it facedown over the *maccheroni*. Slowly remove the paper or foil, and the pastry will fall perfectly into place.

For the crust
    1¾ cups flour
    9 tablespoons unsalted butter, at room temperature
    ⅔ cup sugar
    3 large egg yolks
    Pinch of salt

Put all of the ingredients in a large bowl and combine them using your hands, working the ingredients between your fingertips until the dough comes together. Form the dough into two flat disks. Place on a large plate, cover with a dish cloth, and refrigerate for at least 1 hour.

On a lightly floured surface, roll one of the disks into a circle at least 13 inches in diameter and about ⅛ inch thick. Fit into a 9-inch springform pan, letting the excess dough hang over the edge.

Roll the other piece of dough into a circle at least 10 inches in diameter and about ⅛ inch thick. Put it on a baking sheet and return both pieces of dough to the refrigerator, again covering them with dish cloths.

For the filling
>   2 medium yellow onions
>   1 medium carrot
>   1 stalk celery
>   3 tablespoons olive oil
>   8 tablespoons (1 stick) unsalted butter
>   1 pound ground meat (see headnote)
>   3 cups Emilia's Tomato Sauce (page 5)
>   Salt and freshly ground pepper *a piacere*
>   9 ounces *maccheroncini* or penne pasta
>   2 cups freshly grated Parmesan cheese

Peel and finely chop the onions and carrot. Finely chop the celery. Sauté the vegetables in the olive oil and 4 tablespoons of the butter in a large saucepan over medium heat, stirring, until they soften, about 5 minutes. Add the meat and cook over low heat for 20 minutes.

Add the tomato sauce and salt and pepper, and let simmer slowly for at least 2 hours, stirring occasionally, until the sauce is thick and flavorful. Let cool to room temperature.

Cook the *maccheroncini* in a pot of boiling salted water

according to the package directions until very much *al dente.* Drain, and mix with the Parmesan cheese and remaining 4 tablespoons butter. Set aside to cool to room temperature.

To assemble and bake, preheat the oven to 350°F.

Remove the dough from the refrigerator. Fill the lined pan with half of the *maccheroncini,* top with the meat, and then with the remaining *maccheroncini.* Cover with the top crust. Flute the edges, pinching the top and bottom crusts together and cutting away any excess dough. Prick the top with a fork, and bake for about 30 minutes.

Increase the oven temperature to 400°F and bake for 20 minutes more or until golden brown.

Makes 6 servings

Christmas lunch was served in the vast living room that opened onto the garden, the heavy mahogany center table extended to accommodate all the family members, who often numbered thirty, between uncles, aunts, and their children. My mother's cousins—Fiammetta, Giovanna, and Luigi—arrived from Como with their parents, beloved Zio Corrado and Zia Letizia. I looked at them with unabashed respect and apprehension: older and sophisticated, these cousins seemed to possess a world knowledge that still eluded me, combined with a talent for caustic teasing. Zia Adriana, tall and wiry, made her entrance with Lina and Giampiero, my grandfather's two unmarried cousins. Extraordinarily polite and gentle, they spoke in a strange and graciously archaic way, choosing their words and greeting the various members of the family with the utmost elegance. "*Riverita, Signorina!*

My reverent respects!" Giampiero would say, bending his tall figure and kindly taking my hand in his.

My grandmother's table was transformed into a feast of delicate pastel colors for the occasion. Mamma and Nonna Valentina laid the precious pink and gray china on the beautiful white tablecloth. Pale green crystal glasses were lined up in elegant formations of four at each place setting, exhibiting their different shapes and sizes, ready to be filled with white and red wine, water, and *spumante*. Silver sparkled all over the table, and in the center, a huge cornucopia triumphantly held fruits and flowers. Seasonal yellow apples clustered next to intensely scented Sicilian citrus, and vine shoots of luscious zibibbo grapes cascaded from the borders, with white roses, cyclamen, and one solitary, unexpected iris.

A small round table was dedicated to the children. Here my brother, sisters, cousins, and I sat and ate, free from the inhibiting rules that governed the adults' rituals.

Moments before the Christmas meal was served, Nonno enacted a well-orchestrated entrance into his "personal pantry," a little space off the telephone room where he kept fine foods and wine. Solemnly wrapped in a blue-and-white-striped apron, he would grip a dangerous-looking knife and free an immense Prague ham from its elaborate box and paper wrapping, then carry it out into the living room to a small rectangular table covered with a white lace cloth. There it would sit, in all its terrifying splendor, my grandfather's customary Christmas treat.

Nonno's duty was to slice, as finely as possible, sweet pieces that Cristina then arranged on a large tray and passed around to the cheers of children and grown-ups.

"Ecco qua, il prosciutto di Praga!" he would proudly exclaim, delighted to provide a superb delicacy for his dear ones.

Various *arrosti* inevitably followed the *pasticcio*: large cuts of veal, turkey, and capon slowly roasted in the oven with rosemary, sage, and bay leaves. The meats were arranged on large silver platters, surrounded by a tricolor bounty of sweet peas, tiny baby carrots, and roasted potatoes cleverly cut into small, regular cubes. The simplicity of the menu was only superficial, since the most meticulous care had been focused on choosing every single ingredient. The sweet peas had to come from Antignano, a small hamlet outside Livorno, a lovely strip of land bordering the sea. *Pisellini d'Antignano* were the ne plus ultra of sophistication: sweet as little dots of pure sugar, they literally melted in the mouth.

Panettoni, specially ordered from a Milano bakery, were laid on the side tables, with mountains of *torroni, panforti,* and *ricciarelli,* the traditional Christmas sweets. Silver stands overflowed with offerings of fresh fruits, hazelnuts, walnuts, figs, and dates. Out of superstition, the entire family ate a large quantity of tender, sweet raisins, an essential part of the Christmas and New Year rituals, as they represented good luck and prosperity for the year to come. The zibibbo that graced the silver cornucopia met the same fate: its shoots were stripped by the end of the meal.

No one knew about wine. Bordeaux and Burgundy surely never played any role in our festivities. An adequate Chianti from any well-known producer was indifferently served, and no family member wasted time discussing its properties; we simply drank it. Even children were allowed to have a sip. Like the adults, we had our own wineglasses and, for once, instead of being given a few beads of the precious liquid in a glass full of water, we were allowed to drink a small quantity in its pure form.

The pale winter sun warmed the marble terrace outside the

French doors, and immediately after lunch, they were opened, inviting the numerous members of the family to gather outside. It was time for the annual photograph, taken as we all posed against the empty flower étagère and the naked background of the dormant garden.

IN EMILIA'S KITCHEN

Looking into the dining room

Emilia's circadian rhythms dictated the success or failure of our family lunches and dinners, affecting even the modest afternoon teas and *merende*. When her mood reached fragile, the entire household walked on eggshells. Nonna

Valentina and Mamma exchanged knowing glances and simply disappeared from the range of Emilia's agitated waves.

Meals became sad affairs of insipid broths and overcooked vegetables. Nonna quietly proclaimed *affettati* (cold cuts) and cheese superior to Emilia's uninspired fare, and even my grandfather kept his grumbling to himself, relying on one of his customary Latin proverbs: "*Ut sis nocte levis, sit tibi cena brevis.* To rest well at night, eat sparsely."

Emilia's virtues mostly overcame her occasional periods of psychological frailty. With me, she always displayed incredible patience. The afternoons spent under her vigilant eye learning how to cook were oases of calm, infinitely pleasurable for both of us. We did everything by hand: egg whites were beaten to a snowy consistency with a simple long-tined fork. I admired Emilia's ability to produce the fluffiest mountain of whites in a matter of minutes. I had to stop and rest, moving the fork from my left hand to my right, looking in desperation at the transparent yellowish liquid that sloshed from side to side in the bowl.

An indefatigable Emilia showed me the best way to whip up a perfect *maionese,* slowly stirring the egg yolks and adding the *filino d'olio,* the nearly imperceptible stream of extra-virgin olive oil, to the mixture. It gave it a beautiful viridescent hue. I loved to see the sauce's firmness increasing before my eyes, and feel its growing resistance against the whisk I energetically maneuvered. Incredible what a couple of egg yolks and some olive oil could create!

"*Piano, piano.* Don't be impatient," Emilia ordered.

I sat on a chair, holding the bowl between my knees to keep it from shifting. Following Emilia's precise dictates, my right hand gripped the balloon whip. "Always remember to stir in the same direction. *È il segreto della maionese.*"

Sometimes the mayonnaise suddenly changed color and consistency, turning from a beautiful smooth bright yellow to an alien pale emulsion, sprinkled through with infinitesimal grainy white dots. *"La maionese è impazzita, Bimba!"* Emilia would proclaim.

For me, at the age of seven, it was puzzling to think that a *maionese* could all of a sudden *impazzire* and lose its wits.

"Non impazzire, ti prego!" I whispered to the bowl. "Please, don't go crazy!"

In the unfortunately quite common instance when I caused the mayonnaise's grainy derangement, Emilia made me add a tiny crushed piece of boiled potato. Instantaneously, like magic, the creamy substance returned to normal. I was safe, and the mayonnaise's sheen and sanity were restored.

In the process of establishing my cooking skills, I learned that many sauces run the risk of going crazy. Béchamel tended to *impazzire*, vanilla custard sauce and *zabaione* too. I clearly didn't want to be responsible for the mental health of so many sauces and creams and was terrified at the possibility of causing such a dire affliction.

❧ Maionese ❧
MAYONNAISE

Importante! The egg yolk must be at room temperature. (Please also note that it is raw, and raw egg can occasionally harbor harmful bacteria.) If all of a sudden your *maionese* goes crazy, don't worry! Think about Emilia and simply add a crushed tiny piece of boiled potato.

1 large egg yolk, at room temperature
½ cup extra-virgin olive oil

Lemon juice
Salt and freshly ground pepper *a piacere*

Drop the yolk into a bowl held between your knees. Whisking constantly, slowly add the olive oil drop by drop; always stir in the same direction. If the mixture becomes too stiff, just add a few drops of lemon juice until the mayonnaise regains the proper consistency. Continue stirring until all of the oil is incorporated. Season with lemon juice and salt and pepper.

Makes about ½ cup

Emilia's famous *fagiolini al burro* tasted like no one else's. "*Ma come farà mai?* How does she do it?" everyone asked after tasting the tiny, buttery string beans. The beans had a wonderful savory quality, with an especially appealing aroma. It was impossible to pinpoint the spices she had used to produce that enigmatic blend of flavors.

Behind the scenes, I learned her secret. She merely added a few crumbs of *dado* Knorr. Nothing more, nothing less than a bouillon cube transformed her beans into the distinctive dish everyone praised. She boiled the beans and then quickly sautéed them in butter, adding the bouillon that turned into a delicious golden sauce. I instinctively knew not to reveal the truth, and I kept this interesting piece of information under wraps to protect Emilia's universally admired talents.

Emilia performed many fascinating tricks, marvels of creativity bestowed on us for good behavior. She taught my sister Giovanna to make miniature cakes, delightful hills of immeasurable gratification, to serve to her dolls. Giovanna simply filled Emilia's sewing thimble with a spoonful of chestnut flour and water and placed it next to the hot ashes in the wooden stove. The result was almost immediate; the thimble turned hot and the mixture inside became solid. An expert tipping of the impromptu mold, and my younger sister had a perfectly proportioned miniature work of culinary art in her hands. We all clapped and devoured the tiny cakes, after a superficially generous offer to her dolls.

Gorging on chestnut flour, which was kept in a brown hemp sack on the pantry shelf, was one of my passions. After weeks sitting in the winter humidity, it developed *gnocchetti,* hard little lumps of gray sweetness. Closing the pantry door behind me, I proceeded to eat forbidden handfuls, filling up my mouth with a gluey substance that slowly melted, releasing its unbelievable sweetness. Sometimes I panicked. What if the flour suffocates me? I worried, anxiously checking my breathing. But a gentle masochism of the culinary senses prevailed and I continued, undeterred, to stuff my mouth.

I loved crouching on the pantry floor between the chicken food and the bags of rice and pasta, surrounded by familiar smells. My head barely reached the shelves stocked with wonderful food: fresh and dried fruit, jams and preserves. I closed my eyes and gave free rein to my nose and olfactory imagination.

"*Mi sembri un cane da tartufi.* You resemble a truffle dog," Nonna often accused when I inelegantly sniffed every vegetable, herb, and fruit that passed under my nose. I loved the scent of fermented golden apples—the only ones permitted to my diabetic grandfather—and the decadent essence of the ripening persimmons, and the gaminess of prosciutto. I sniffed the musky aroma of the olive oil kept in an ancient jar. The chipped rim had taken on a greenish hue, stained by many years of ladling the oil into the everyday bottles. Potatoes just dug from the garden, dusty and dirt encrusted, still retained their earthy odor. I indulged in the penetrating vinegary smell of *sottaceti,* the pickled vegetables Emilia prepared in September.

Nonna Valentina hated to cook. As a child, she had been forced to learn the secrets of good housekeeping. At the beginning of the twentieth century, marriage was all an Italian girl could hope for, and Nonna's family considered it her ultimate goal in life. For the necessary apprenticeship, Valentina's well-intentioned, stern *zia* Bianca prescribed daily sewing, embroidering, and cooking drills. *"Chi non sa fare, non sa comandare"* was the often-repeated sentence. "If you want to give orders, you must know how to do things yourself."

The only girl in a family of eleven children, Nonna had lost her parents at the age of eleven during *la Spagnola,* the terrible influenza epidemic of 1908. Her childless aunt and uncle, Bernardo and Bianca Fabbricotti, opened the doors of their beautiful house in Livorno to Valentina, while her ten brothers went to live with different relatives.

The Fabbricotti mandated that their young niece learn the ways of becoming a lady. Promptly, home economics classes started, with cooking lessons first. Valentina's governess wrapped the young girl in a large apron to cover her dress, and downstairs she went. The tediousness of learning the minutiae of basic cooking paled only in comparison to the stultifying evenings she spent playing chess with Zio Bernardo in the starched silence of Villa Fabbricotti.

Despite those uninspired beginnings, Nonna grew into a talented housewife, particularly good at putting together menus and deciding on recipes to be realized by her skillful cook. Before World War II, she gained fame as an elegant entertainer, planning wonderful dinner parties and afternoon teas with her friends. Her *salotto* attained the highest prominence in social circles.

While my grandmother preferred to *dare ordini* than cook herself, she nevertheless taught me many recipes. That she was not a devotee of the culinary arts took nothing away from her expertise.

I listened while Nonna showed me how to make *zabaione* the old-fashioned way. Modern Italian kitchens had already acquired some time- and labor-saving appliances, but not ours. "*Sta tutto nella mano.* It is all based in your hand," she explained, introducing me to *il frullino,* the little wooden utensil that ended in a star. "*Guarda!* Squeeze the handle between your two palms and try to make a uniform rotating movement." With her hands, she demonstrated the motion, advising ways to minimize the fatigue that eventually afflicts even the most exuberant twirler. Stirring and whisking were tiring jobs. Inside the pot, though, the little star created its magic. Twirling slowly inside the casserole over a very low flame, *il frullino* transformed eggs and Marsala wine into a perfect *zabaione,* the delicate dessert cream that everyone loved. "*Sta attenta che non impazzisca.*" Once again I had to deal with the curdling malady. Piqued, I paid more attention than usual, and my first *zabaione* emerged in full golden glory. I lovingly plunged my spoon inside the cream, lifting it again to admire the way it fell back in thick yellow streams inside the bowl.

"We could add a couple of drops of coffee to transform it into an even better treat," Nonna offered.

"*Si, per piacere! Caffè.*" I quickly adopted her suggestion. Flavored with strong coffee, my new masterpiece metamorphosed into a sophisticated adult dessert.

✿ *Zabaione al Caffè* ✿
COFFEE ZABAIONE

Remember, always whisk in the same direction, and *state attenti che non impazzisca!* Nonna would serve this in individual crystal cups, with wafers.

- 1 large egg yolk
- 2 tablespoons Marsala wine
- 1 tablespoon sugar
- 1 tablespoon strong coffee

Fill the lower half of a double boiler with an inch or two of hot water. Put the egg yolk, wine, and sugar in the upper part of the double boiler. Put the pan together, set over low heat, and start whisking the mixture. If you happen to have a *frullino,* twirl on! Otherwise, a balloon whip will do. The mixture will slowly change appearance, first frothing, then rising, and finally becoming thick and ribbony. At this point it is ready; add the coffee and serve immediately.

Makes 4 servings

Like all self-respecting castles, Emilia's fortress—the kitchen—had a resident ghost, a larger-than-life spirit named Reali, who occasionally antagonized her. In Villa Fabbricotti, where my grandmother grew up, Reali had earned everyone's respect by running sternly and properly—for at least thirty years—the imposing house with a large staff. Many years after his less than hasty departure from this world, my family continued to whisper his name in reverence: "Reali, *ah!*" A passionate gastronome, he had scrupulously noted his favorite dishes, documenting decades of kitchen culture, in an impressive culinary log. *Le Ricette di Reali* was our family's gastronomic bible.

When Mamma and Nonna decided that one of Reali's famous delicacies had to be realized, they would barge into Emilia's kitchen and inform her that they were going to prepare some dish or another. Though the doors to the Highest Culinary Knowledge were about to open to reveal Gastronomic Truths, Emilia would react unfavorably to this threat to her culinary integrity. It was almost as though the tall, imposing gentleman had physically violated her kitchen. Emilia's lips tightened into her trademark thin line of disapproval, her arms folded defensively across her chest, and an I-am-going-to-sabotage look appeared in her eyes.

The recipes, dating from the beginning of the twentieth century, included *pasticcio di fegato* (liver pie) and *lingua salmistrata* (brined tongue). The latter—Reali's most celebrated dish—was the best example of the inherent generational and cultural gaps. "All you need is to get hold of a big piece of tongue," read the tidily written recipe. Once that elongated, charcoal-gray slab of meat rested on our kitchen table, Mamma and Nonna—the enthusiastic followers—had to "beat it with vigor and then work it with saltpeter until it becomes soft under the hand." The raw *lingua*, thickly covered by raspish black skin, was to be left on an inclined plate for twenty-four hours to drain all its liquid. "The secret factor in this case is brine," Nonna excitedly informed my mother, reading the recipe aloud from the red notebook. The essential step entailed boiling salt, vinegar, sugar, bay leaves, and peppercorns in a pot of water.

"Throw an egg inside the boiling liquid, and if it floats, it means that the salt-to-water ratio is perfect," Reali's notebook continued. "Leave the tongue covered with brine for a whole week. The liquid has to cover the meat fully and after seven or eight days, the dish is finally ready." Emilia's eyes rolled up to the ceiling, while she hissed her usual supplication to a plethora of saints to infuse her with patience.

"When it has produced a lot of foam, the tongue is done," Mamma read. These words elicited my personal sound track of grossed-out cries, which only increased at hearing Reali's further instructions on cleansing, boiling, and skinning.

"Flay the skin in just one fluid movement," the butler suggested. I eyed that inert abhorrence, hiding behind Emilia, who shuffled around the kitchen passing the appropriate tools to Mamma and Nonna like a disapproving nurse during a botched surgery.

The via Roma garden was a self-contained Eden. Fruit trees hovered over sumptuous flowerbeds and tidily clustered lines of calla lilies. Pear and peach, apricot and persimmon, medlar and fig trees lived comfortably next to elegant shrubs, radiant rose bushes, and dazzling multicolored dahlias. They democratically shared the limelight with brilliant show stealers such as the intensely scented gardenias and camellias that grew in large terra-cotta pots behind the magnolia, toward the end of the garden.

Outside the kitchen, immediately to the right, a wall ran for several feet. Along its length, orange and mandarin trees thrived, growing against the warm ocher bricks, which retained the sun's intensity till the end of the day. The slightly elongated, dense-skinned oranges belonged to a special variety. Their sharp taste made us cringe. Not for nothing were they called *aranci amari,* bitter oranges.

On any given January day, when the oranges were at their brightest gold, Mamma might suddenly metamorphose into a maniac. We never knew when she would strike. Then, having mutated into a despotic general, my gentle mother would announce: "Today we will make *la marmellata d'aranci.*" Mamma summoned Paolo and me to help pick the oranges. While we collected a huge harvest, much of the fruit still fell to the ground, bursting into a splashy mess. The pervasive sharp citrus scent attracted millions of bees, ants, and even a cuckoo bird, who moved into the last tree at the corner of the vegetable garden.

Once the cartloads of oranges were safely brought into the kitchen, the time-consuming marmalade making would start. The kitchen was transformed into a laboratory, with everyone lending a hand to clean, peel, cut, stir, measure, and taste.

"Make sure you wash them really well," Mamma ordered, showing her troops how to scrub the fruit of any residual dirt.

"They must cook for a long time." She instructed Emilia to make sure to simmer the whole oranges for at least an hour and a half.

Once the oranges were soft enough to puncture easily with a toothpick, Mamma put them aside in a large bowl, covered to the rim with cold water. The water needed to be changed quite often over a period of at least two days. "It will take care of their bitterness, wait and see. *L'ha detto Peggy,*" Mamma explained. Peggy Anderson, who lived in a beautiful villa not too far from via Roma, was a childhood friend of my mother. English and thus a jam expert, she had passed on the recipe, establishing our winter family ritual.

"*Si! Che bello!*" I exclaimed when the two days had expired and I could help separate the rind from the useless pulp. Emilia passed down to my end of the table the oranges cut in precise halves and I then excavated the water-whitened insides. A bowl received the peels, while the flesh was thrown into the garbage. For each kilo of rind, Mamma added one and a half kilos of sugar, and once again set the pot on the stove to simmer.

An intense smell—sharp, sweet, and zesty—filled the kitchen for days, assailing my nostrils and making them twitch with pleasure as I savored the combination of citrus and slowly cooking sugar.

"*Deve diventare color dell'oro!* Stir it regularly, until it becomes the color of pure gold!" Mamma repeated year after year.

Another of Mamma's specialties that I particularly loved was candied orange peels, their bitter taste counterbalanced by their sugar coating. During the marmalade-making process, some of the best rinds were collected in a special pot, where they were boiled for a few minutes. As soon as they had reached a perfect consistency—firm but succulent—they were rolled in a big tray lined with sugar. The little white grains sharply transformed those wrinkled rinds into elegantly contorted shapes, immediately sweet to the palate, but with a tangy aftertaste that always left my taste buds begging for more.

Sometimes my mother would dip one end into bitter chocolate, but that particular flourish was sparsely indulged, since chocolate belonged to the rarified category of Expensive Pleasures to Be Enjoyed Frugally.

✀ *Marmellata di Aranci Amari* ✀
BITTER ORANGE MARMALADE

2 pounds bitter oranges, thoroughly scrubbed
4 cups sugar

In a big pot of water, simmer the whole oranges for at least 1½ hours, until they can be punctured easily with a toothpick. Drain the oranges, transfer to a bowl, and cover with cold water. Let sit for 2 days, changing the water twice a day during this time.

Drain the oranges and cut them in half. Scoop out and discard the pulp, placing the peels in a large pot. Add the sugar and set the pot on the stove to simmer over medium-low heat. Cook, stirring occasionally, until the marmalade thickens, about 35 to 40 minutes. The marmalade is ready when it has turned a rich, dark orange.

Fill clean (or sterilized) glass jars and seal according to the manufacturer's instructions, or refrigerate for up to 1 week.

Makes about 6 cups

At twelve, I started to experiment with recipes offered by the various women's magazines, like the renowned *Cucina Italiana*. My first "real" recipe, where I actually had to follow written instructions, was *mele al cartoccio* (apples wrapped in pastry). I loved the concept, impressed by the pictures of beautiful fruits wrapped in a thin layer of buttery dough and baked in the oven until they glistened in their golden coats. The fact that these apples were served on a sparkling silver tray and set on a splendidly decorated table was part of the appeal. A little footnote modestly hidden between the ingredients and the cooking time read: *"Cordon Bleu* recipe." Having seen *Sabrina* with Audrey Hepburn probably five times, I knew that the *Cordon Bleu* label exerted profound cachet beyond the kitchen, imparting lifelong lessons of style and comportment. First, it was imperative to wear sleek black tapered trousers while cooking. Second, it was indisputable that French Cooking School training would ferret out a Humphrey Bogart. Third, when you cooked French dishes, Edith Piaf automatically started singing *"La Vie en Rose"* in the background. I boldly jumped into my newly found Gallic passion. The recipe was a success, proving the Latin saying *Audaces fortuna adiuvat.* Fortune certainly does favor the bold, as I received much adulation from my loving family.

"Patrizia ha la mano giusta per la cucina. She really has a touch for cooking," Nonna and Mamma proclaimed proudly and soon promoted me to a position of greater responsibility. "Patrizia, I am giving a *dopocena,* would you prepare one of your specialties?" became a frequent request. My mother loved inviting friends to these after-dinner parties, as they were an economical and elegant way to socialize involving the preparation of only cakes, drinks, and *caffè.* Since I was the staff, there was no overhead either. One of my specialties was *il dolce di Nonna Giovanna,* Nonna Giovanna's cake: several layers of coffee-and-rum-soaked biscuits lavishly spread with a delicious creamy filling of butter, strong coffee, and sugar. That same cream covered all sides, with the added touch of chocolate shav-

ings to grace the top. In Italian it was aptly named *una mattonella,* for it indeed looked like a brick. This cake was part of my paternal grandmother's legacy and, while focusing on the slippery butter that never wanted to combine with *caffè,* I would remember my long-since-gone Sicilian *nonna.* The ingredients resented their forced alliance, dark coffee drops skating all over the satiny yellow mound of butter, trickling down the sides, finding refuge in the far corners of the mixing bowl. Eventually I got the upper hand in this uneven match, discovering, by chance, that I simply needed to warm the *caffè* before forcing it into the butter.

Livorno's wonderful vegetables proved to be much easier ground for culinary experiments. Emilia's teachings and our excursions to the market left their imprint. "*Bimba,* when you select fennel, you must remember to buy the female ones, as they are fatter and less stringy," she would instruct while examining the bulging white stalks. Her fingers touched and measured, instantaneously selecting the unblemished exemplars that qualified for *la tavola dei signori.* I spent innumerable days trying to understand her recommendation, but this gender hand-picking continued to remain a mystery to me. How could I ever recognize the male from the female? In despair I looked at the feathery green plumage that adorned them: Was it possibly a distinctive sign? Maybe the female ones had longer plumage? I was never right.

One of Emilia's most successful dishes and one of my favorites was *finocchi e porri al forno,* fennel and leeks covered with butter and Parmesan cheese and baked until golden but juicy. While speed and good results didn't always go together in my kitchen education, in this case they did, so I often had the satisfaction of preparing this plate all by myself. It became my forte.

✳ *Finocchi e Porri al Forno* ✳
BAKED FENNEL AND LEEKS

Emilia was right: it is important to choose the "female" fennel bulbs; they must be fat and firm. Always select perfectly white fennel bulbs, as a change in color usually means that they are old.

    3 fennel bulbs
    4 medium leeks
    ½ cup flour
    8 tablespoons (1 stick) unsalted butter
    1 cup freshly grated Parmesan cheese
    Salt and freshly ground pepper *a piacere*

Bring a large pot of water to a boil over high heat.

Trim away the base and the feathery leaves of the fennel bulbs and cut them lengthwise into 8 wedges, discarding the outside layer of leaves. Wash them. Salt the boiling water, add the fennel, and cook for about 5 minutes. Drain, pat dry, and set aside for the moment.

Cut off the base of the leeks and trim away the darkest green parts. Pull off the first two outer layers and discard. Thinly slice crosswise with a sharp knife. Put the leeks in a colander and wash them thoroughly under running water. Drain well and pat dry.

Preheat the oven to 375°F.

Coat the fennel with the flour, shaking off the excess. Arrange it in a lightly buttered 12-inch ovenproof serving dish.

Sauté the leeks in 3 tablespoons of the butter in a medium sauté pan over medium heat for about 5 minutes, stirring, until they are translucent. Scatter them over the fennel. Cover with the Parmesan cheese, season with salt and pepper, and dot with the remaining 5 tablespoons butter.

Bake for about 25 minutes, until the top is golden. Serve hot.

Makes 6 servings

WASTE NOT

Mamma and Nonna

The war left my family feeling precarious, no longer belonging to a world of certainty; the simple daily routine of running a household would never again be taken for granted. They saved everything. Used rubber bands, fragments of old gift paper, multicolored bits of ribbon, stubs of pencils, and pieces of erasers graced the drawers of every piece of furniture in the family house. "One never knows when it might come in handy," Mamma and Nonna would explain whenever pressed to throw away their precious possessions. One of the most famous examples of family thriftiness was my great-aunt Letizia, who kept a box labeled: *SPAGHI. Troppo corti per essere usati.* (STRINGS. Too short to be useful.) The loss of beloved possessions started what we later called the War Syndrome.

Because of its strategic position on the Tyrrhenian Sea, with its thriving port and naval academy, Livorno had become an important target for the Allied bombers. My family was displaced when the Germans invaded, their house allocated to a regiment that destroyed, stole, or ruined many precious things. The soldiers vandalized all the furniture, new and antique, severing legs from chairs and tables, demolishing woodwork, slashing upholstery, and shredding curtains. Each book from our library, to the last volume, had been thrown casually from the second floor windows to stoke the great bonfires that roared on the marble terrace.

Paolo and I often heard of the hunger that plagued our family during the last years of the war, when they lived with relatives in Cernobbio, a quiet mountainous area near Lake Como, far from the battlefields.

Zio Guglielmo, my grandfather's older cousin, somehow always managed to get hold of jars of strawberry jam, cookies, and exquisite white bread through the black market. But he and his wife ate these delicacies in front of their nephews and niece without ever considering that their starved audience might become almost mad with craving, until the day disaster struck and my grandmother decided to intervene.

One afternoon my mother's younger brother, Pierluigi, at that time only thirteen, could no longer resist the powerful attraction of jam, and he tiptoed into the kitchen to eat a spoonful. Just one drop fell on the floor. A few hours later, pandemonium broke out when the evidence of the theft was pointed out to his mother by her self-righteous relatives. Valentina cast aside her usual self-control, and blasted her cold fury at Guglielmo and his wife. "Don't you have any pity? Don't you see how starved the children are? We are all enduring rationing, and you feast in front of us. Where is your heart?"

Unfortunately, she failed to elicit Zio Guglielmo's contrition. Instead, he retreated to his room carrying the precious jars, the cookies, and the fragrant white bread. He locked the booty in his chest of drawers, muttering "*Siamo vecchi*. We are old and should lack nothing."

Another evening, still during the war, the entire family—my grandparents, and my mother and her younger brother, both still in their teenage years—sat down to a surprise at dinner. There was meat on the table! *Un miracolo* almost impossible to grasp by a family accustomed to rationing and scarcity. The big vermilion hunks of meat swam in tomato sauce on the plates, tempting everyone. They all ate it with great haste, uttering sounds of inordinate pleasure. My mother and her brother were astonished. Grandfather too was smitten. How could they be eating meat?

Nonna Valentina started singing quietly, *"Clippete-cloppete-clop,"* to her puzzled audience. Forks and knives had by then swept the plates clean. She sang, *"Clop-clop-clop,"* for a few more seconds until comprehension finally dawned on the faces of her family.

Many years later, when her wide-eyed grandchildren heard the story, they exclaimed: "Nonna! *Che schifo!* How awful! How could you ever eat a horse? Did you devour an entire one?"

Born in 1948, I never experienced the hunger my grandparents and parents had endured, but my siblings and I were constantly reminded of how lucky we were to find food on our table. *"Mangiate tutto; pensate ai bambini poveri.* Eat everything on your plate; think about the poor children who have nothing." I resented those children for a large part of my childhood. They were responsible for my having to eat codfish, for my having to finish scraps of meat with myriad disgusting veins and fat apparently invisible to the adults. The same culprits accounted for unwillingly ingested bowls of minestrone soup: daunting pieces of *cavolo nero,* the local black cabbage, floating in a mysterious well of unrecognizable chunks of dark vegetables. With my nostrils offended by the strong smell, I disconsolately plunged my spoon into the bowl, hoping for a miraculous tornado that would carry the soup away from the table, directly to *i bambini poveri.*

Minestrone

The secret of a good minestrone is to gather a great variety of green and leafy items; proportions are not particularly important. Each time you make minestrone it will be different, according to the predominant ingredient. There is no need to trim the greens: the long cooking time takes care of tough stems.

To "Waste Not," you can serve minestrone in many ways: the first day, ladle it directly over a piece of toasted bread rubbed with garlic; the next day, process it until smooth before serving; the third day, add cooked *pastina* or crushed spaghetti when you reheat it. Always serve minestrone with freshly grated Parmesan cheese and extra-virgin olive oil.

Minestrone freezes extremely well; I always freeze several one-portion containers to use whenever I need them (even if I might need four at once).

1 large yellow onion
1 large carrot
3 tablespoons extra-virgin olive oil, plus extra for
      serving
About 3 pounds mixed greens, such as spinach, cabbage,
      kale, Swiss chard, and/or *cavolo nero* (Tuscan black
      cabbage)
About 1 pound mixed vegetables, such as zucchini,
      broccoli, and cauliflower
1 large potato (any kind)
One 14-ounce can crushed tomatoes
A Parmesan rind (if you have it)
Salt and freshly ground pepper *a piacere*
Freshly grated Parmesan cheese for serving

Peel and chop the onion and carrot. Sauté in the olive oil in a big pot over low heat, stirring, until the onion softens, about 5 minutes.

Meanwhile, clean and slice the greens and other vegetables: Cut the greens into thick strips. Cut the vegetables into 2-inch pieces. Peel the potato and cut it into big cubes.

Add the greens, vegetables, potato, and tomatoes to the pot, and pour in water just to cover. Bring to a boil, then lower the heat to the minimum. Add the Parmesan rind and salt and pepper. Cover the pot and simmer for as long as possible: I usually allow between 4 and 6 hours.

Remove the Parmesan rind before serving—unless you

have a child who likes to eat it (Emilia always saved it for me).
Sprinkle each portion with Parmesan cheese and drizzle with
olive oil.

Makes 8 servings

Growing up, I had to obey the many laws of "Waste Not" that
ruled the house. First was that lights never be kept on when not
needed; we were constantly reminded that "electricity costs."
After having flipped off the white porcelain switch in my room,
I would run as fast as I could to reach the safe area of the fully lit
living quarters, rushing to trade menacing shadows for the soft,
comforting light and warmth of the kitchen.

For most Italians at the time, central heating was a fantasy, but
our house was one of the very few to have a built-in heating system. In the thirties, a huge coal-fed boiler had been installed in
the basement directly under the kitchen. A system of pipes crisscrossed the interior of the walls of the house, blowing hot air into
special sliding vents in every room. Once the system was turned
on, the ascending hot air rapidly heated the entire house.

Paolo and I considered the delivery of the coal one of the
week's most entertaining events. A tiny window—almost a porthole—in a cubicle adjacent to the boiler room opened directly
onto the street, and through it the mountains of coal cascaded
directly into the basement. Accompanied by a thunderous rum-
ble, the coal was funneled from the horse-drawn truck through
the porthole, forming an enormous pile in the cellar. Clouds of
black dust rose through the window gratings, permeating the
bushes that half-hid the "portholes" on the garden side and

wafting throughout the basement rooms. Emilia kept my brother and me at bay, allowing us to watch but preventing us from approaching the tantalizing mountain of wicked blackness.

We loved to look at the coal man and his horse. They wore the same expression, resigned to their dusty fate, placidly tolerating the slow pace of their job. We imagined a strong symbiosis between the man and the horse as they lifted feet and hooves in unison, solemnly shifting their weight from left to right, waiting for the coal to reach its destination.

Because coal cost a fortune, my grandparents kept the heat down to a spartan minimum. Individual stoves became the answer to our diminished circumstances, a perfectly practical way to warm up just one room at a time.

Throughout the day, Emilia made almost continuous trips to the basement. She laboriously descended the steps behind the kitchen, toting the long-beaked coal scuttle. Her small stocky body had started to weigh heavily on her legs, slightly hampering her mobility. Nevertheless, up and down she went, carrying the coal to the various rooms, feeding the ever-ravenous black stoves. *"Madonnina mia!"* she uttered at the top and bottom of the precipitous staircase. Leaning against the wall, she would rest her reddened hands on her thighs, breathing hard.

The beak of the coal scuttle fitted nicely inside the mouth of each "Warm Morning," as the English stoves were appropriately called. It was a good way to translate all that grimy blackness into pure comfort. Still, the house remained terribly cold in winter. I spent many days and nights studying in my frigid room, wrapped in shawls and sweaters of varied provenance. Their appearance notwithstanding, the ugly expanse of knitted brown horrors, salvaged from ancient sweaters discarded by my elegant grandfather, provided a welcome and cozy protection.

Counteracting the bitter cold inspired many ingenious strata-
gems. The attic housed several trunks that had somehow escaped
the German invasion. Built of solid dark brown wood ringed by
beautiful metal ribs, they nearly burst with real treasures: pieces
of fabric, yarn, tiny fragments of old lace. *"Prima o poi servi-
ranno.* Sooner or later they will be useful," pronounced my frugal
nonna. There were also several pieces of fur pelts: minks and the
grim remainders of a small African animal called a dik-dik, which
had been shot in Kenya by my grandfather at the beginning of
the century. Downstairs, in the second-floor drawing room, a
huge tiger and a lion lay in wait for us; their enormous heads
hard as rocks, their teeth permanently displayed in macabre
grins that never failed to attract our probing fingers.

My practical grandmother came up with the brilliant idea of
sewing together several of the mink pelts, thus producing a most
spectacular fur blanket to cover my crib. In the gloomy Livorno
January of 1948, I must have looked like a Hollywood baby, so
luxuriously protected against the *Libeccio,* the strong southwest
wind that swept unforgivingly through the town, bending the
strong pine trees and twisting the willowy tamarisks. Its insidi-
ous drafts invaded the house, seeping through the old windows,
insinuating itself under doors.

Since the winter was so bitter that year, I needed more than
just the mink blanket, and Nonna Valentina came up with
another spectacular idea. Taking the impeccable white flannel
tennis trousers that had belonged to my grandfather, she cut
them into perfect squares to be stitched together. The result was
a strikingly elegant receiving blanket, a soft patchwork of
immaculate whites with which to swaddle the little baby who
had arrived amid severe but dignified scarcity.

But by the time I was ten—between the hand-me-downs from

the rich Como cousins and my grandfather's recycled trousers—I was dressed endlessly in blue dresses and skirts. A couple of times a week, Bibi, the seamstress, would come to our house to spend the entire day sewing dresses, smocks, shirts, and bed and table linens in the so-called armoire room. Bibi extolled the virtues of the blue flannel fabric to my mother: solid, everlasting, practical. Mamma eagerly agreed: "Bibi, look at these trousers! We can make them into a skirt for Patrizia. *Sono perfetti.*"

An enormous table in the center of the room supported mountains of laundry ready to be starched and ironed. Draped with a long white cloth that reached the floor, this table quickly became my "home." My brother and I spent endless afternoons cocooned underneath it, reading and playing cards. My mother, in splendid moments of complete understanding, served us great *merende* of sliced bread and butter, generously sprinkled with sugar. I loved feeling the smoothness of the table's underside, interrupted by the dark nails that dotted the boards here and there. Our fingers traced endless scribbles in the dust in one of the few places it found refuge from Emilia.

When I was thirteen, my mother regrettably decided to bestow upon me the honor of wearing those famous dik-dik pelts. We reverently brought them to the local furrier to be transformed into an elegant garment. But when the svelte coat was produced, my problems started: it shed everywhere—on me and on whomever was sitting, walking, or standing anywhere close to me. It was mortifying to walk through this haze of hairy dust. Lavishing teenage boys with flying beige fur did nothing to advance my social life. "*Hai visto quella lì?* Have you seen her? She must have some kind of disease!" my classmates sneered, exchanging glances. The coat quickly found its way to the farthest recesses of my wardrobe.

We always wore skirts to school, never trousers. It was not considered proper for a young girl of a good family to look and behave like a boy. Other girls my age dressed in a fashion I much admired. Their large skirts, made of multiple triangles of fabric cut on the bias, danced attractively around their young legs, while my stiff blue skirts simply hung, shrouding any human shape. Though I had learned during catechism that envy was a mortal sin, I abundantly sinned, day after day, on my way to school and at all the parties I attended.

A fashion photograph I had seen in one of my mother's magazines showed a beautiful model languidly resting on a red velvet chair in a marvelously gilded theater. With relaxed sophistication, she wore one of those flared skirts, and a pair of the most sharply pointy-toed shoes I had ever seen. Instantly, my great goal became to possess these icons of high fashion. At the first opportunity I had to buy a new pair of party shoes for my ever-growing feet, I insisted on acquiring the same kind of flat *ballerinas* in black patent leather. *"Per piacere, Mamma! Ballerine con la punta!"*

These shoes had such a sharp point that the abstract concept of torture became painfully tangible. And, though irresistibly enchanting, this footwear produced no social magic.

For weekend parties, our large group of friends met in the old garage of dark-haired and extremely handsome Stefano, whose family had generously transformed the space into a kind of club. The large doors opened directly onto the garden, allowing for relaxed wandering into the romantic darkness of the graveled paths. The omnipresent rose bushes and the balmy Mediterranean pines silently witnessed many hot teenage romances. The record player regaled us with endless hours of wailing Paul Anka songs, Neil Sedaka's sorrowful laments, and the cutting-edge vibrations of Elvis Presley's provocative guitar. Unfortunately, not the very coveted Stefano, or the highly lusted after Pietro, or any of the other objects of my futile fantasies ever thought for a moment to start a conversation with me or—God forbid—invite me in my chic pointy shoes to dance. I sat permanently next to the turntable, picking up the arm at the end of each song to change record after record, a faithful vestal to the sacred fire of my friends' romantic successes.

Having devoured all available English romance novels, I understood that I had fallen into the undesirable category of wallflower. And whose fault was this heartbreaking catastrophe? I blamed my dresses—of course!—with Bibi, the Como cousins, and my family all coconspirators in my social failure. Certainly it was not due to my skimpy, flat-as-a-board body, or the painful shyness that prevented me from smiling at any of the boys.

Despite the lean times, Nonna Valentina could still create a world of fantasy. Paolo and I—and later on Giovanna and Giulia, my much younger sisters—benefited from her wonderful sense of whimsy and her ingenuity.

In Livorno, it very seldom snows. This lack of meteorological fortune is accounted for by what our geography books call a temperate climate. So snow was material for dreams and, when it did appear, for jubilation.

On the garden side of our house, a large white marble cornice ran under the second-floor windows. My grandparents' bedroom windows opened over that cornice. On those rare occasions when it snowed, Nonna Valentina invited her grandchildren into her bedroom to watch her prepare the *"canarino gelato."*

She put a straight line of elegant, tiny crystal glasses outdoors on the marble shelf. The snow filled them, falling silently and unhurriedly in front of our eyes. We spent long hours watching it accumulate. Only when the glasses were full did Nonna pick them up, place them on a tray, and add a few drops of sweetened lemon syrup or the juice of a freshly squeezed orange.

"*Bambini, è pronto.* Here comes *il canarino gelato.*" Nonna Valentina dragged us away from the window and gave each of us our tiny chalice, a spoon, and all the freedom that pure fantasy can unleash in a child. We were eating the most elegant dessert in the world. After all, it had come down from heaven.

"*Mai mangiato niente di così buono?*" We nodded knowingly to each other. "Have you ever eaten anything so exquisite?"

⚜ Canarino Gelato ⚜
CANARY SORBET

First, pray that it will snow. Then, put a glass outside on your terrace, windowsill, or garden and wait until Mother Nature fills it. Next, squeeze in a few drops of juice from a freshly squeezed orange. Last, have your children understand that this is a really special treat!

Il Convento
del Sacro Cuore

Il Convento del Sacro Cuore class picture;
author is in second row from top, sixth from left

My grandmother's prediction, uttered when I
was still a toddler, became a well-known family axiom: "*Luciana,
questa bambina ti farà vedere i sorci verdi*. This baby will make
you see green rats." My sweet mother had unknowingly produced an unpredictable child and was in for a number of sur-

prises. In a well-calculated move, I was sent at the early age of five (instead of the customary age of six) to the Convent of the Sacred Heart, my exhausted mother's way of disposing of her endlessly energetic daughter for a few hours a day.

Apart from being the best school in Livorno, the convent was also conveniently located on via Roma, just a few meters away from our home. Consequently, after the first weeks, I walked to school all by myself, with great pleasure and pride. My mother followed my progress from the balcony on the second floor, leaning out over the balustrade to watch me until I disappeared, not always enthusiastically, inside the convent.

My first teacher was Sister Agnese, a gentle woman and a very good instructor. Nevertheless, I hated the interminable first months of *prima elementare* (first grade) painstakingly spent covering pages and pages of graph paper with pothooks and straight lines. We had to use a pencil to learn the discipline of drawing insignificant alien signs. My eyes got lost in an expanse of gray sticks that had to be traced from the page's top line, shooting straight down without exceeding the allocated space.

"It is the secret to beautiful penmanship," Sister Agnese repeated every time she caught her pupils fuming with frustration, struggling laboriously.

Then, several weeks into the gentle Tuscan spring, when all the classroom walls and windows were decorated with paper swallows, yellow cardboard chicks, and intensely perfumed daffodils, the nuns finally initiated us into the perilous world of writing in ink. Serious problems were just about to start.

Our class was furnished with traditional two-student desks with shared bench seating and a footrest. Set into the wood of each desktop was a white porcelain inkwell; to its left, another little porcelain container collected the discarded quills. Our pens rested in a groove next to the inkwell.

In our schoolbags we carried an important accessory: *l'astuccio*. The rectangular wooden box opened via a sliding lid to reveal a world of interesting articles and gadgets. Divided into several sections of various lengths and widths, it contained all we needed for a day of learning: erasers, pencils, pens, and the little nibs individually wrapped in paper that required careful handling. Each nib culminated in two funny converging halves, slightly rounded, which were not supposed to overlap. Many of them ended up in the defunct-nibs container before they even had a chance to draft a perfectly rounded consonant.

"*Attenzione, bambine!* A perfectly straight tip is the correct way to begin our class," Sister Agnese repeated, mantra-like, to her slightly nervous pupils. We certainly wouldn't want frightful ink marks smudging the pages we filled with armies of As and Bs . . .

Once we had safely secured a nib into our pens, Sister Agnese made the tour of the classroom, adding a few drops of ink to each well. We then plunged our pens into the inkwells, carefully eliminating any excess ink by gently touching the borders of the containers. We were finally ready to write.

The maddening chaos of drops, splashes, sprays, and splatters that ensued wreaked havoc on our most diligent work. By the end of each school day—around one o'clock—our spirits had sunk low, but energies were running high. Something had to be done to reestablish the entertainment quotient, and on one fateful day I decided that this task lay in my hands. I bent toward the girl sitting directly in front of me, ominously close to my desk and its inkwell. Temptation was too strong. I plunged—just once!—the tip of one of her braids into the indelible black ink and then let it go. It slowly returned to its owner's back and the immaculate white smock that covered it, trailing intricate splotches that surpassed any ink blots created for a class project.

I ended up with my first disciplinary call to the Mother Superior's office. But the smudgy results of my act filled me with perverse pleasure. As early as first grade, I was already doomed to membership in the club of undisciplined students.

Once I'd acquired the pleasure of deciphering written words, I spent subsequent years immersed in books, regularly disciplined for being found guilty of reading too much. "*Spengi la luce!* Switch off the light! Stop reading! Sleep! It is late." With great confidence, I disobeyed the strict orders of in-bed-and-asleep-by-eight; I simply brought a flashlight to bed and read to my heart's content under the blankets.

One night I dared a little too much. When my mother came to check whether Paolo and I were asleep, she saw a great deal of commotion under the covers. That night I'd secreted not just the usual book and flashlight but also a French dictionary, to try to finish the engrossing novel I had begun with Nonna Valentina, *Les Malheurs de Sophie* by La Comtesse de Segur. Naturally, the frequent word searching in the large dictionary added a suspicious bustle to the usually calm reading activity. "*È mai possibile?* Do I always have to repeat the same admonitions?" Mamma exclaimed, eyeing me in complete disbelief. Swift confiscation of all incriminating tools ensued.

One afternoon, my grandmother and I found ourselves sitting together in the little drawing room on the second floor. Immersed in *All Quiet on the Western Front* by Erich Maria Remarque, she occupied the large armchair covered in a warm burgundy red damask; I sprawled, in my ill-mannered habit, on the small sofa nearby.

I was reading *The Good Earth* by Pearl Buck, discovering for the first time the marvels of China. I wanted to see with my own eyes the pagodas and the temples, the courtyard houses with the rounded moon gates, and the elegant ladies transported on palanquins. My galloping imagination sent me across the countryside, entering humble huts and visiting elegant villas. I walked on soft rugs that muffled the sound of my cloth-clad feet. I touched the embroidered red curtains protecting the rich ladies' alcoves. I visualized the golden temples, their mysterious darkness filled by the imposing statues of Buddha. I dreamed of lighting incense sticks to the ancestors' tablets.

Nonna and I were each so transported by our reading that we forgot about the passing hours, turning the young afternoon into a gentle evening. The sun had relinquished its pink hue; oblique rays filtered through the green shutters, golden particles of light floating in from the garden. Yet we remained unaware of any change in the afternoon luminosity.

Emilia tiptoed upstairs. "*Ma Signora,* at what time would you like to have dinner?" We looked up, startled, and quickly checked our watches. It was already past the usual dinnertime. Carefully closing her book and placing it on the table, Nonna looked serenely at her eldest granddaughter and spoke words that I have kept in my heart since then: "To be able to share silence is the greatest sign of friendship and love." The sheer pleasure of sharing a morning, an afternoon, an evening with a loved one, while reading a book, is an experience that unites more than a thousand spoken words.

In the fifties, Italian schools opened in October. This meant September preparatory rituals. In the saccharine way of those days, the RAI, the national radio, would announce that "the young Italian students are ready to go back to school, like the swallows who crowd the telephone and electrical lines, preparing for their trip to warmer climates." I never understood this comparison. No logical link existed between us and those lucky birds that flew away to Africa.

Visiting *le librerie,* the Italian bookstores, was the best part of back-to-school preparations. The distinct odor of paper, books, and stationery enveloped me as soon as I entered the store, a sweet mixture of sandalwood, pencils, and India rubber and ink, musky and piquant at the same time. We bought, en masse, erasers, fancy pencils with rubber tops, an extra supply of nibs, a new *astuccio,* and all the paraphernalia needed for schoolwork. One of the best possible acquisitions was *la gomma-pane,* an extraordinary eraser that looked exactly like a lump of bread dough. Soft and pliable, the *gomma-pane*—rendering validity to its name—possessed the added quality of a sweet scent, something between organic heaven and intoxicating oil products. Its claim to fame derived from its ability to erase ink marks in a matter of seconds and with relative ease.

Blotting paper was another important element in the writing process. The huge soft white squares, carefully cut into manageable sizes by our loving mothers, saved our newly learned vowels and letters for posterity. The *carta assorbente* in time became an important accessory to games. My friends and I sent each other complicated messages that only a mirror could decipher, and I felt more clever than Sherlock Holmes when I clandestinely raised my grandfather's blotting paper to a mirror to translate the garbled backward words into somewhat comprehensible prose.

"*Egregi signori,* by virtue of this present letter I entrust to you. . . ." The Italian business lingo looked cryptic even with the mirror's wizardry. I shook my head in disbelief. This was what the adults wrote?

Once home after our bookstore blitz, my mother set out to cover every book with strong brown packaging paper, the only way to ensure a decent lifespan for my new sources of erudition. Nonno's studio on the second floor was dedicated to such activities. Mamma would spread paper over the reading table and then start her patient work of accurately cutting, adapting, folding, and taping. Our multicolored books metamorphosed into nondescript brown parcels, individual distinctions evident only by the titles applied in Mamma's large elegant handwriting. The books aligned neatly like the RAI's October swallows resting on telephone lines. Once again, school was about to begin.

Among the nuns at the Convent of the Sacred Heart, Sister Jacopina was the "dragoness" who taught catechism. She possessed a really scary huge foot, permanently encased in a bulky brown leather boot, as a result of some mysterious disease. She limped heavily from class to class in the desolate dark corridors of our school, producing an ominous *thud-thump, thud-thump, thud-thump* that reverberated from wall to wall.

Needless to say, I hated her classes. Not only was she a nasty woman, but her corpulent frame exuded an intense smell of unwashed body parts. When she bent over my desk, the huge stiff white veil that covered her head encircled me. The wimple around her chin held back some of the offending odors, only to release them in concentration whenever she stretched her powerful neck.

During our daily home economics lessons, we had to learn embroidery. Sister Jacopina informed us that we had to use up our

threads to their complete ends. If we didn't, we would suffer forever in hell. "*L'Inferno* is waiting for you!" she added porten-
tously. The same burning fate would befall us if we dared to use
only part of our writing pads, since we were supposed to cover
every square centimeter of every single page. She regularly told us
gruesome stories of marble Virgin Mary statues embracing unre-
pentant sinners in cold, deadly squeezes: "*La Madonna* slowly
opened her arms and crushed him!" Our eyes widened in horror.

I didn't like her threats. Marble Madonnas didn't seem likely to
squash people. But not wanting to risk my young soul so prematurely, I obeyed, covering my notebook's sheets to their maximum
capacity and embroidering to the last usable millimeter of thread.

My school was not for the faint of heart, as I learned when
Mother Superior died. Sister Giacomina was very old and, for us
in the elementary classes, very mysterious. The day after her not-
so-unexpected demise, we were asked to come early to school to
pay tribute to her saintly life and to pray in front of her casket.

We walked into the chapel's nave wearing our white smocks,
white lace veils covering our heads. Mother Superior, in all her
shriveled smallness, was propped up on a fancy trestle, lying in
the middle of a forest of white lilies, callas, daisies, dahlias, and
chrysanthemums. We circled in an unbearably slow line around
her bier, praying and chanting, while stealing quick glances at
her fragile remains. I was surprised by how dark her face looked
and by the number of wrinkles crisscrossing her long face. Suddenly I was overtaken by a terrible fear. In my first meeting with
death, I considered that maybe Sister Jacopina was right after all!
We were nothing but walking bodies inhabited by immortal
souls. What, then, if her stories about the killer Madonna proved
equally accurate? I went home horrified and spent several nights
haunted by nightmares that materialized into wild screams.

* * *

Beginning at age six, we all attended classes six days a week, from eight in the morning until one in the afternoon. Italian schools traditionally didn't offer lunch, so as soon as the bell rang, hundreds of us found ourselves on the street looking for something to eat.

Thankfully, Livorno street food was magnificent, one treat better than the next and all conveniently located near our school. The most famous was *la torta di ceci,* a twenty-inch-wide razor-thin pancake made of chickpea flour and olive oil—nothing more, nothing less. The amber batter is spread in a thin layer in a large iron pan, then baked in a wood oven. After a few minutes, *la torta* emerges—golden, crisp, and fragrant—ready to be sliced.

A specialty of Livorno, this dish is impossible to replicate successfully in other cities or regions. *"La vera torta di ceci la si trova solo a Livorno!"* as any Livornese worth his name will cry.

The formidable hunger that normally squeezed our stomachs at about noontime caused a collective catapulting into the little pizza stores. Our ink-spotted fingers stretched anxiously toward the counter at La Rinomata Pizzeria Seghieri Elio—my favorite temple of indulgence—and our ravenous young mouths uttered precise orders: *"Un cinque e cinque, per piacere."* It was the magic code for five liras' worth of *torta* and five of bread. Whenever I had enough money, I joined the group, pushing and shoving to reach the counter where *la signora* Seghieri expertly sliced *la torta* into narrow wedges with a deft movement of her right hand, holding the enormous flat iron pan with her left. The mountains of soft *pagnotte,* made with pizza dough, slowly started to diminish. She picked up one and sliced it in half, slipping the *torta* wedge inside, then quickly wrapped it in yellow paper. *"To'eccoti!"* She handed it over to me.

✣ *Torta di Ceci* ✣
CHICKPEA PANCAKE

I am sure yours will taste as good as that of the Livornesi! *Signori* Seghieri used big professional round pans. I simplify and use a jelly-roll pan.

> 1¾ cups chickpea flour
> 4 cups water
> Salt *a piacere*
> ¼ cup extra-virgin olive oil

Preheat the oven to 400°F. Lightly grease a 16 x 12-inch jelly-roll pan or rimmed baking sheet.

Put the flour in a bowl and slowly stir in the water, making sure that there are no lumps. The mixture will remain quite liquid, like pancake batter. Season with salt and stir in the olive oil. Spread evenly in the pan.

Bake for about 20 minutes, until golden and crisp. Cut into large pieces and serve immediately.

Makes 8 servings

✣

"La fame muta le fave in mandorle! Hunger makes hard beans sweet!" wrote Dante in his *Paradiso*. In our case, it was not just

hunger, as Livorno's fast-food quality reached the pinnacle of gourmandise. Hunger also quickly made us forget our good manners as we shoveled the food down our throats.

Next on the List of Great Snacks came *gli scagliozzi,* tiny firm rectangles of polenta quickly fried in hot olive oil. Sold by weight at only a few liras each, *gli scagliozzi* kept piping hot for a long time, performing in wintertime the dual task of warming both hands and stomach. Whenever I indulged in the luxury of street food, the filling, earthy food so appeased my appetite that home-prepared dishes lost their appeal. "*Bimba,* how can you fill yourself with that?" Emilia fumed, bitterly witnessing my refusal to eat her lovingly prepared *pasta al burro.*

Castagnaccio is another wonderful, traditional Tuscan peasant food, so easy to make that anyone could turn it out in ten minutes. Its main ingredient is chestnut flour, to which cold water is gently added until it becomes semiliquid, at which point pine nuts, raisins, and a few drops of the best olive oil combine to enhance the flavor. Sometimes a little branch of rosemary, its pungent smell well married with the sweetness of the flour, studded the hazel surface of the pancake. When chestnuts were picked and stored in late fall, little stands would crop up at every street corner, in front of schools and churches. Semisweet, tender, and distinctively nutty, *castagnaccio* is in itself worth a trip to Tuscany in fall or winter.

Castagnaccio

CHESTNUT PANCAKE

4 cups water
2 cups chestnut flour

Salt *a piacere*
¼ cup extra-virgin olive oil
2 tablespoons raisins
2 tablespoons pine nuts
1 sprig rosemary, if you have it fresh (do not bother to
   use dry)

Preheat the oven to 400°F. Lightly grease a 10-inch round cake pan.

Mix together the water, flour, and salt in a bowl, making sure there are no lumps. Spread the mixture into the greased cake pan. Drizzle with the olive oil, and sprinkle with the raisins, pine nuts, and rosemary, if using.

Bake for 40 to 50 minutes, until a toothpick inserted in the center comes out dry. Cut into wedges, and serve immediately.

Makes 8 servings

The convent offered its own treats, capitalizing on its captive audience of famished little girls. In the tiny pantry behind the church, off the long corridor that led to our classrooms, *Suor* Jacopina sold, dearly, miniature pastel-colored sugar eggs filled with cream, red sugar strings, and tiny licorice candies. The shiny plump blackberries were another of my favorite choices, little sugar dots that melted deliciously in my mouth and left a fabulous chemical aftertaste that lasted for several minutes.

For once *Suor* Jacopina was responsible for her pupils' lightheartedness. No marble statues, no eternal infernal flames could interfere with her nifty profit. Gluttony, when bringing liras to the convent's coffers, was highly commended.

My memory of Confession is not particularly flattering to my immortal soul, and it certainly betrays my already secretive young mind. I had discovered something pleasurable, and I knew enough to try to hide it. Prompted by some stimulating glimpses of *National Geographic,* which portrayed naked people in faraway tribes, my "discovery" involved lots of thigh squeezing but no touching at all. An unexpected and wonderful pulsating warmth soon permeated my entire body. The feelings were confusing and overwhelming.

A vague sense of guilt and embarrassment made me wonder if this activity was not exactly appropriate. After all, our religious education dictated that physical responses of this magnitude were neither encouraged nor approved. Were my actions an affront to God? What to do?

I knew that whenever we did something wrong, we had our fabulous way out. Confession would absolve all of our sins through the infinite love and compassion of Jesus Christ, our Lord and Savior. But could I really describe those surprising physical details to the priest?

A brilliant solution, provided indirectly by my grandfather, emerged. In his youth, Nonno had picked up a little Swahili during several wonderful years in Kenya, and he had taught us some useful words. The one that fitted perfectly into my scheme was *matacco,* meaning "bottom." I decided to try it out. I went to Confession feeling a little apprehensive, but ready to venture forth with my budding ability as a polyglot.

Father Metello, the wonderful Franciscan friar who took

charge of our souls, waited for us once a week in the serene dimness of our school church. That afternoon, I filed into the chapel together with my classmates and we waited, patiently and piously, on the benches. We genuflected and looked impressively focused on our saintly state as Perfect Little Catholic Girls. I entered the confessional and began: *"Confesso a Dio Padre Onnipotente . . ."*

Among the many venial sins that had plagued my week—I had talked back to my mother, I had kicked my brother, I had refused again to eat breakfast—I slipped in as innocently and casually as possible that I had "played with the *matacco*." I held my breath waiting for the sword of God to descend upon my mortal body in swift punishment. After a pause, Father Metello's gentle voice inquired, *"Nient'altro?* Anything else, my child?" As usual, he ordered several Hail Marys and a couple of Our Fathers to cleanse my soul completely. And there I was, free again.

The fashionable side of First Communion appealed to me more than the spiritual side of the Blessed Sacrament. I longed for the white dress, coveting the precious veil that would cover my head and qualify me as another tiny "bride of Christ." I dreamed of walking down the aisle of the church, taking small pious steps exactly like the nuns when they filed in for High Mass in their hierarchical formation.

One of the most important honors conferred on those who made their First Communion was the invitation to walk in the large procession of the Pentecost, a Catholic Holy Day of Obligation devotedly celebrated by the Livornesi. The prospect of participating in such a theatrical production was greatly alluring. I would be dressed once again in the long ceremonial gown with the white shoes and elegant thin socks. I would walk all over town, looking beautiful and attracting appreciative smiles.

I felt the pressure of my importance weighing on my young shoulders long before the actual procession day, when my entire class would congregate inside the imposing Basilica of Santa Maria del Soccorso. I savored the pleasure of leaving the cool dark nave, slowly following, step by slow step, the multicolored flower petals that lined our route. Sweet Madonna faces ethereally sketched in thousands—no, millions—of rose, carnation, and dahlia petals. The houses flanking the streets would exhibit outrageously colorful silk banners of inspired themes: popes, with their eyes emphatically rolled up, gazing heavenward; Christs with long blond beards and bleeding stigmata; velvety purple hearts; and luminously haloed white doves embroidered over golden skies.

"Nonna, how come the Holy Spirit is a pigeon?" I would ask her. "*Bimba,* don't be blasphemous."

Fantasizing about the procession was enough to fill the empty space between my mother's goodnight kiss and my blessed sleep.

While I was never a particularly pious child, there were moments when a little bit of saintliness managed to brush off on me. The month of May was dedicated to the Madonna, the famous *Mese Mariano.* During these weeks, Sister Agnese kept on her desk a crystal bowl filled with white pieces of paper, little virgin notes that were just waiting to record our *fioretti. Fioretto,* means literally "little flower," an "act of mortification, a small sacrifice made for devotion." By dedicating to Maria a daily *fioretto,* we celebrated the Mother of Jesus.

"*Bambine,* write down your *fioretti!*" Every morning we approached Sister Agnese's desk to pick up the blank pieces of paper on which to inscribe our tiny paradigms of goodness, and every morning we had to think hard to come up with a new good deed for the day. We intently scribbled our acts of generosity on the tiny pieces of paper, then folded them into thin rectangular shapes, tied them in loose knots, and replaced them in the crystal bowl.

As could be expected, the process degenerated into a small war of inventiveness. Who in our class would make the best and most devoted act? By the middle of the first week of May, it was already difficult to be imaginative. Famous for my competitiveness, I was severely stressed at the beginning of every spring, trying to conceive of new and clever sacrifices.

Each day Sister Agnese selected some of the anonymous *fioretti*. Though no one knew the identity of the authors, curiosity transfixed every girl to her tiny chair. Sister Agnese then proceeded to unfold the papers slowly and read aloud their devout content.

"Ma che bello! A child has donated her afternoon snack, her *merenda,* to the beggar outside her home. This is very good!" The great compensation—or disappointment—was the reaction of the classmates. The "Oh!"s and "Ah!"s of the other girls were the barometer that measured the success of these mini-martyrdoms. Mine were often committed to self-betterment. For example, I would, with extreme suffering, lend my coloring books to Paolo or voluntarily offer to embroider some perfectly hideous cushions. A couple of times, for want of something better, I even volunteered to ingest without complaint a plate of revolting *baccalà,* the awful dried cod regularly presented to us on Fridays. Accompanied by dejected-looking potatoes, the dried-out white fish emanated a powerfully fetid smell. This particular *fioretto* was not repeated many times, because violent retching was usually the unfortunate consequence of this specific act of piety.

During those beautiful last days of May, the acute perception of school ending intoxicated us; summer holidays were just around the corner, bringing with them the salty breeze of endless sunny days and the transparency of the Tyrrhenian Sea. The culminating moment of the school year occurred, appropriately, on the very last day of the month. The entire school, resplendent in starched and carefully ironed uniforms, assembled in long, disciplined lines. Bright blue ribbons, tied in billowy bows, bobbed under our chins. Our solemn faces showed our eagerness to celebrate the Feast of Good Behavior.

The nuns headed the procession. Mother Superior was at the head of the line, with the rest of us behind, starting with the nursery children. Immediately after came the unruly elementary and middle school girls, finally closing with the old and wise seventeen- and eighteen-year-olds. The older girls wore black uniforms without ribbons, eliciting much envy.

We sang the *"Salve Regina,"* we belted out *"Ave Maria."* We recited prayers to the Madonna while slowly inching our way through the park, our long line winding up to the ilex grove where, in a small clearing, the marble statue of the Virgin of the Sacred Heart stood. The narrow gravel paths that crisscrossed the school garden crunched and crackled under our feet. Lilies, white and strong, with their topaz pistils, erupted everywhere, flaunting their rich perfume and purity that have been for centuries an integral part of Catholic iconography. Dahlias of every kind clustered in Technicolor masses, while minicarnations in the softest shades of pink nearly overwhelmed the entire garden with their sumptuous perfume. Red, yellow, pink, and white roses, in their most brilliant end-of-May display, punctuated our solemn advance toward the statue, their fragrance adding an almost disturbing poignancy to our purpose.

"Salve Regina, Mater Misericordiae. Vita, dolcezza e speranza nostra. Salve!" Once we convened around the statue, we contin-

ued to chant for a while, expressing our unwavering faith through the small *voci di testa,* the "head voices" that the nuns had taught us. Not only was it a great pleasure to find those thin notes hidden *inside* our heads, it was almost physically gratifying to make them explode into the sunny air of a perfect May morning. It certainly was another auspicious step toward achieving the famous sainthood to which we aspired.

The climatic event was when the Mother Superior and the nuns knelt in front of the Madonna and burned the mound of paper *fioretti,* sending up thin ribbons of smoke to shroud the gentle face of the Virgin Mary. Flames and smoke, the everpresent symbols of purity in almost all cultures, transformed those May mornings into a near-pagan ceremony. We restored our Catholic credo by reciting endless rosaries between hymns.

GARDEN LESSONS

Nonna Valentina in the garden

Tall walls covered with climbing vines and plants enclosed our garden. The east wall, lined by a long row of luscious orange and lemon trees, ended abruptly at a corner. There the garden continued in a giant L shape where, during the war, my grandmother had planted a vegetable garden.

Unruly ivy and a big elder tree (where an old cat, blessed by nature with extraordinary striated orange fur, found permanent refuge from his meowing peers) concealed the gray cement walls.

An ancient gnarled pear tree, planted almost half a century before by my great-grandmother Saffo, swayed from under the elder's shade, trying to catch some of the sun's rays. The combination of shade and sun must have been perfect, because the little tree produced the best fruits, firm and juicy.

One of the climbers occupied a particularly special place in my heart. The simple campsis, or trumpet vine, *Bignonia grandiflora,* year after year presented us with a generous crop of magnificent red flowers. My family named it *La Pianta della Tartaruga* (the Tortoise Plant) because of a new inhabitant of the garden, an independent creature with a mind of her own, that Paolo and I had discovered one day. The beautiful tortoise would appear and disappear regularly—to our great happiness or disappointment—according to the circumstances and the seasons, but we never really knew when she would spend time with us. My brother and I fed her lettuce and other green leaves to show our hospitality, hoping to buy her gratitude and affection. We had been taught that she hated winter and chose to retreat into lethargy during those long tedious months. Though hibernation was a new, interesting concept, Paolo and I persistently attempted to convince the tortoise to stay with us permanently. One day we tried a new delicacy, offering her one of the trumpet vine flowers. The little rumpled head darted out from her variegated brown shell, and her mouth, a thin straight line of wrinkled determination, gradually twisted into a grin of gluttonous delight. She devoured this bizarre new delicacy and expectantly waited for more tortoise caviar. "*Guarda, Nonna!* She likes it!" my brother and I exclaimed.

Under the auspices of an amused Nonna Valentina, Paolo and I began to strip the campsis climber of all the flowers on its lower branches, to just about the height we could reach, given our age and size. Every day we searched for the reddest, most perfect trumpet flowers to offer to the garden's special guest, but the unflappable tortoise continued to vanish into her hiding place. In the end, our schemes did not triumph over the lure of her time-honored winter siesta.

This particular plant, in fact, turned out to be heaven for all sorts of insects and animals. Maybe it was the attractiveness of its flowers, with their elongated corollas that opened up into the eccentric trumpet shape, liberally flaunting their sexy coral petals. Insects of every size and strength sooner or later seemed to find their way into the campsis's inner secrets. The scariest one was a huge hornet, black and hairy, with great large wings that produced a frightening polyrhythmic noise when flying. My brother and I emitted high-decibel screams at the mere sight of the black beast. As soon as the hornet soared by, zooming and gliding through branches and leaves, we dropped our toys and ran desperately toward Nonna and Mamma. *"Aiuto, Aiuto!"* we shrieked, our unrestrained hysteria storming through the afternoon peace. Our screams were sometimes sufficiently frequent to summon my grandfather, furrowing his white bushy eyebrows, to the window of his library. My mother and Nonna Valentina were horrified at the commotion we had caused.

One day Nonna, determined to put a halt to such ruckus, patiently called us to the table just outside the large marble terrace near the living room windows. Both my grandmother and mother always sat there, doing something—knitting, embroidering, or sewing. Reading a book was considered such a treat that it was usually confined to the afternoon hours, after the daily duties had been completed.

Nonna drew us to her knees and started to explain: "These insects are not dangerous at all. They are just *creature di Dio*, and God's creatures don't intend to harm you. Patrizia and Paolo, don't worry and especially do not scream. Am I clear? Do you understand me? You have nothing to fear, the poor insects are simply enjoying their day, exploring bushes and pollinating the garden's lovely flowers. *Andate a giocare adesso.* Now go play," she added with a smile.

Holding hands, obedient and angelic in our neat overalls, we nodded, happily reassured, and returned to our games. But a couple of minutes later, another big black hornet suddenly swooped by on his way to the campsis vines, and Paolo and I once again ran back to the safety of our mentor's knees, this time wildly screaming, *"Una creatura di Dio! Una creatura di Dio!"*

An explosion of laughter echoed through the garden. Mamma and Nonna were in hysterics, tears running down their cheeks. The phrase was quickly adopted and introduced into the family lexicon, and from that afternoon every hornet was invariably called "a creature of God."

The high walls separated our garden from the neighbors' properties. To the left of our house was a family with two children, our great friends Anzino and Margherita. Anzino's real name was Hans, because his father was German, but my fellow Livornesi transformed its pronunciation into a much more comfortable Italian version. Hans was Anzino to everyone.

The wall between our gardens was in some parts replaced by an elaborate iron grating, covered with dense ivy. Close to where the grating met our house was a natural opening in the greenery that the four of us quickly transformed into our play area. Our daily activities in this corner further depleted the lusciousness of the ivy, resulting in a substantial hole. But though the vines looked mangy and threadbare, we had established a more comfortable space for our games, and here we played with one

another for hours and hours, separated by solid iron bars: Paolo
and I on one side, Anzino and Margherita on the other.

We invented a number of wonderful games. One was called *"Il
Circo delle Formiche,"* a sort of Barnum and Bailey with ants.
Together we built a magnificent circus, complete with trapeze,
tents, rings, and balloons, and featuring clowns and a ringmaster.
It was completely made out of Pongo, a pliable multicolored
"play-dough" to which we were thoroughly addicted. Paolo and
I always asked *Papà Natale* to bring it at Christmas and also
requested it as a present for our birthdays. Everyone, including
Santa, generously complied, but, as usual, rules were attached.
We had only a very few specific places where we could enjoy our
favorite pastime. Because Pongo left indelible stains on every
unprotected surface, it was never allowed inside the house, and a
strict "no Pongo" rule was enforced on the marble terrace as well.
So we retreated to the wall opening, with Anzino and Margherita.
Only there could we manipulate the colorful blocks, kneading
them into shapes, persons, and objects.

Who were the circus performers? Who climbed our trapezes
and hustled over bridges and trampolines? *Le formiche*, of course!
We would pick them up in the morning, when the poor unsuspecting ants were going about their daily business near their
anthills. We then transferred them into the tiny, specially built
Pongo houses.

"And now! Here they come! The greatest ants in the history of
the circus! Ladies and gentlemen, look at them! In their black
stretch suits, performing the most difficult exercises in the
world." The ants, oblivious to our screams and incitements, scurried up and down the ropes and trampolines, hoping to find a
way out. Once we finished the game, we carefully took the unfortunate insects back to where we had found them.

Near the garage where the gravel was thicker, we played *le biglie*. We owned several beautiful little glass marbles in the most intense pastel colors. When they rolled, their cores spread colorful rays of light all around. The marbles came in little mesh bags with string closures. They had become collectors' items, and we were seriously passionate about their appearance and features.

Reflecting the national passion for *ciclismo*, Paolo and I traced large tracks through the gravel in twists and turns, uphill over the grass and precipitously downhill, in rings that circled the *Souvenir de la Malmaison*, the exquisite rose my grandmother favored. With our *biglie*, we organized intense and aggressive equivalents of Giro d'Italia or Le Tour de France, naming our marbles after the famous champions of the fifties. "Go, Bartali! *Forza, Coppi!*" we shouted with all our lungpower, while excitedly watching our little *biglie* roll to success or complete defeat.

The game was an exercise of prowess and rigor: Kneeling on the ground, we positioned the marbles at the start of the track. Taking turns, we then propelled them forward, flicking them with index finger against thumb. It was not easy, since the little spheres tended to tumble out of their designated route at the first misguided flick. But how satisfying to push our cyclists to the top of the Dolomites or the Pyrenees and finally come to the finish line! Though the game was very competitive, its beauty was that it could be played by just one person or by many children at the same time. *"Binda ha vinto!* He won!" I jumped up and down, celebrating my champion *biglia*, who had triumphed against the vast field of no one.

Our sexual education also began at the opening in the ivy. One day Anzino declared that he knew something so interesting and so important that we would all be left in awe and amazement. But he was going to tell only Paolo. Anzino started whispering animatedly with Paolo. My younger brother listened with rapt concentration, looking adequately impressed until I saw a look of bewilderment pass across his face. "Really?" he kept repeating. "Are you sure? *Non è vero!* I can't believe it!" Paolo shook his head in total astonishment, but continued to nod. "This is the most surprising piece of information, a real eye-opener. *Grazie,* Anzino," he thanked his friend, eyes sparkling with a neophyte's enthusiasm.

I couldn't wait. I had to know. As soon as the conference between the two boys ended, I abruptly dragged my little brother away from the wall opening and ruthlessly trapped him against the corner of the house. "And now you tell *me,*" I hissed between clenched teeth. "I am your elder sister and you owe it to me. Otherwise . . ."

Paolo blurted: "It is simply amazing! I know how children are born, but it is so incredible that I can't figure out how it happens in real life."

"Come on, tell me. Now. Immediately."

"Anzino swears that babies are born via . . . *il dito!*" Paolo gushed, showing me his index finger, perplexity darkening his gentle blue eyes.

"*Il dito?*" I echoed in total disbelief. "It can't possibly be! Which one? How can a baby fit inside one of these thin fingers?"

We spent a couple of frustrating days studying our hands, slowly waggling them, looking at them from all sides, fanning our fingers in front of our eyes. No openings, nothing. Anzino's information appeared impossible, yet very, very intriguing. The more we considered the situation, the more the involvement of fingers seemed extremely remote. Our baby sister, Giovanna, could never have come out of one of Mamma's fingers.

We decided the only intelligent course of action was to go straight to our mother to shed light on the subject.

Walking up two flights to our mother's bedroom, we intrepidly incited each other. "*Le diremo tutto.* We will tell her everything. Let's see if Anzino is right. After all, he is our age, how can we trust him completely?"

Mamma sat in front of the beautiful old Art Deco mirror that occupied a great part of the wall near the window. An intricate hand-painted vine shoot entwined with delicate pink roses decorated one side, plunging all the way to the bottom, fading away inside the borders. I loved to see my mother combing her hair or dressing framed by this beautiful antique furniture. She was completely unconcerned with her looks, solely interested in wearing well-fitting and appropriate clothes, never allowing herself to experiment with creams and makeup. But her dark chestnut hair, her incredibly fair complexion, and her periwinkle-blue eyes overshadowed her bashfulness. She was simply an unwilling knockout, much to the great amusement of our father, who loved to witness her blush at any compliment.

Paolo and I rushed into the room, startling Mamma with our materialization in one of her few moments of repose, and informing her that we had an important subject to discuss.

"Mamma, Mamma! Anzino told us that Giovanna was born from your finger!" We reported the entire story and admitted that we couldn't make any sense of it. Our mother laughed and told us to sit down.

"I am going to tell you everything." She then started to explain in simple but exact and loving words how nature delivers babies into this world. A slightly different version from the one we had heard just a few days before . . .

Paolo and I looked at each other, comprehension finally dawning. "Ah! *Adesso si!* Now, yes!" Anzino had in fact informed Paolo that babies were born out of the *tito*—our code word for "penis"—but my brother had understood *dito*. The mystery solved, Paolo and I, ages seven and eight, suddenly felt much more sophisticated than our peers, proprietors of greater knowledge.

We sauntered downstairs, skipping steps two by two. *"Il tito, il tito!"* We laughed.

At the southwest end of our property, near the garage and next to the aromatic herb patch, grew our beloved magnolia tree, the focal point of our life in the garden. Shaped like a giant umbrella, it had a mighty trunk, and its evergreen foliage covered a large area with cool, mysterious shade.

Around it, other smaller bushes had been planted to guarantee almost complete isolation from the external world. Juniper bushes with their shiny black seeds and snowberry shrubs with their intensely green foliage grew impetuously in a dense mass. I loved the bizarre milky snowberries, perfectly round, almost transparent, and ready to pop satisfactorily between my fingers. When I wasn't squishing them, I carried them in a satchel and pretended that they were money for shopping in my imaginary stores. My mother supported this flight of fantasy, amused to see her daughter following in her footsteps. Those white and black berries had in fact served as hard currency for two generations, with no devaluation or appreciation. A millionaire in berries, I acquired the fanciest clothes, decorated my room with splendid furniture, and boarded airplanes and boats to exotic destinations. I bought dreams and built castles in the air.

At the end of spring, the enormous magnolia flowers would suddenly burst forth. One day the elongated ivory buds were hermetically sealed, and the next morning prodigious velvety flowers had opened up, splendidly white against the dark cobalt green foliage and spreading their intoxicating perfume throughout the garden. Once fallen to the ground, the large petals metamorphosed quickly into a kind of yellow parchment that rolled up like a scroll, hiding the long stemmed pistils within. I carefully collected these petals, intending to extract the elongated seeds caged inside, whose dried tips had by now turned black. The petals were my matchboxes and the seeds the matches of my make-believe kitchen. With them, I lit my stove, ready to cook delicious meals for hundreds of friends. I fired great ovens, baked wonderful *pizze,* and, as the great chef I dreamed of being, prepared the best *manicaretti* (gourmet dishes) for my grateful family of dolls and stuffed animals.

Under the magnolia's extended shade, I read and read through the summers. There Paolo and I listened to Nonna's tales, tuning in to her with fascination. She would read us our favorite book, *Ciondolino,* which taught us about the life of insects. Ciondolino was a lazy boy who didn't want to study and instead sat for hours in his garden, envying the carefree, simple life of ants and bees, spiders and butterflies.

"On one fateful summer day," Nonna read, "our young hero was admiring the frenetic dashing of a beautiful bee among the inner marvels of roses and jasmine.

" 'How I wish I were a bee!' Ciondolino exclaimed with passion."

At this precise moment, by enchantment, his wish was granted and *poof!* He became a yellow bee with the most beautiful gauzelike wings one could imagine. Our attention was riveted by Nonna Valentina's lips. Not wanting to miss a single word, Paolo and I sat a little more upright, waiting for the succulent details of life in a beehive. We had already guessed what was going to happen, but our hero's problems were yet to start.

"Nonna, tell us about his shirt. What happened to his shirt once he became a bee?" In Italian, *ciondolino* means "something dangling," and in this case it was a well-earned nickname, since Ciondolino was a very untidy boy. A piece of white shirt always seemed to materialize between his jacket and trousers.

"This young bee was different from his colleagues," Nonna Valentina continued. "Under his waist, just at the onset of the black and yellow lines, there was something strange, a little white speck that vibrated in the wind. The other bees were very surprised, but nonetheless showed him his new duties. Poor Ciondolino was relegated to a life of intense labor bordering on slavery."

Our hero had to obey the strict laws of bee life. Solid work from dawn to sunset marked his daily hours; he produced honey and wax, attended the queen, and took care of the many larvae. Back and forth he went, between dahlia and daisy, through the saffron hollyhock pistils, immersed in the lilies' whiteness, covered in golden pollen.

" 'What a life,' he eventually whispered with desolation. 'I wish I could just go back to my old school.' "

And *poof!* By magic, Ciondolino found himself back in his class, where he was finally able to appreciate the positive aspects of school.

The story continued, describing the organized, exacting lives of other insects. Ciondolino, oblivious to his past experiences and regularly refusing to do his homework, endured several other transmutations, much to our delight.

Naturally, by the end, Paolo and I breathed a sigh of relief at finding ourselves still alive as real children, with our homework and few other duties to attend to. "We are really lucky!" we whispered while checking all the spiders and their webs, searching for a little triangle of white emerging from a waist.

The magnolia shaded a round table, whose heavy gray marble top rested precariously on its pedestal and was liable to tip over if one didn't pay close attention. Instead of fixing it, my family kept it exactly like that for my entire childhood, warning repeatedly, *"Attenti alla tavola!"*

During the good season, at about four in the afternoon, Emilia would carry our snacks on a large wooden tray she would set on the table. We kept at a safe distance, patiently waiting for the distribution of the satisfying *merenda:* large glasses of orange juice for the children and a comforting pitcher of iced tea, full of freshly picked mint leaves, for my mother and Nonna Valentina. We devoured in a flash the huge crispy slices of bread coated with yellow butter and sprinkled with sugar.

Occasionally Nonna Valentina and my mother prepared my favorite treat, *l'uovo sbattuto.* This simplest way to conquer a child's heart required just an egg yolk, beaten with sugar to a creamy, marvelous texture. Sometimes the golden delicacy was sprinkled with cocoa powder or even a little bit of ground coffee. I enjoyed the sight of the tiny specks of dark powder dotting the satiny surface and often attempted to insert my spoon without disturbing the harmony of colors and texture. It was the perfect snack—quick, nutritious, and healthy (at that time we didn't worry about *Salmonella*)—a humble everyday version of the adults' sophisticated *zabaione.*

Now and then the everyday *merenda* gave way to more elaborate productions. My family placed scones at the highest level of its Best Afternoon Treats chart. This ranking started with the procession of English nannies who had first taken care of Nonna

Valentina as a child. When scones appeared, it was a ritual for us all to sit listening reverently to our grandmother's instructions.

"Make sure you cut the scone into two perfect halves. *Patrizia, attenta al coltello!* Careful with the knife! The real treat would be to spread clotted cream, but nowadays we simply don't have it. Butter will do, for now."

The war had changed the geography of the garden and its uses. Far away from the house, at the very end of our property, stood a utilitarian chicken pen where there had once been an elegant greenhouse. A great part of the old building had been destroyed by the troops occupying our house, who had entertained themselves, it seemed, by aiming and shooting their guns at the beautiful old glass panels. In the ensuing years, my grandparents tried to clear the grounds and repair the damage; nevertheless, Mamma and Nonna always urged us to be very careful when walking or playing in the area. Menacing slivers of glass often resurfaced under our unsuspecting feet.

Ever the pragmatist, Nonna Valentina had instituted, next to the farthest wall, a mulching pile, putting to good use all the fallen leaves, cut grass, and old branches collected by the gardener. The by-products of Emilia's cooking (bones, inedible nut shells, tough pods, and hard fruit rinds) also accumulated there daily, adding to the immense mountain of yucky things. The mulch ultimately fertilized plants and flowers, undeniably with great results, given the abundance of roses, fruits, and vegetables harvested from our garden.

The intense smell that accompanied the slow decay of nature at its worst, and the danger of glass splinters, made that part of the garden a seldom-visited area. Knowing that a plethora of disgusting insects and animals had elected this garbage kingdom as their permanent residence deterred us as well. Jet-black cockroaches scurried among rotten leaves and decomposed materials; immense moths wrapped their fuzzy dark wings around twigs and oozed a curious white foam from their belly. *"Vedi? È una mamma!"* Nonna called our attention to the disgusting gunk: "These are eggs and will soon produce baby moths." I shivered with nausea.

Nonetheless, our grandmother took advantage of this opportunity to introduce Paolo and me to more natural history. The most interesting to observe were the worms, in all their dark and slimy beauty. What really impressed us was their digestive system. We were told that they feasted on soil and rendered to earth what was of the earth, while enriching it in the process. Every time we accompanied Nonna Valentina to pick potatoes, carrots, or zucchini, she showed us the slow proceeding of the many worms that blessed our kitchen garden, writhing in and out of the fine soil. She pointed out the wrinkly, segmented rings that made their long chubby bodies coil, curl, and twist in such funny ways. *"Sono i contadini della natura,"* Nonna told us. Though they were revered as nature's ultimate farmers, I found them pretty disgusting. When no one saw me, I clandestinely lifted them with a little twig, to avoid contact, and immediately fed them to my favorite chicken. An instant noodle with Bolognese sauce, in just one helping!

I thought that the chicken pen was the best-ever idea and couldn't imagine any other past designation for that building. A net had been raised where glass panels had once protected elegant species of roses and expensive bulbs from Holland. Propped up by wooden rods, it didn't look dignified, but it accomplished its goal, and our family always feasted on fresh eggs and, once in a while, enjoyed the treat of some fabulous chicken broth.

As we say, *"Gallina vecchia fa buon brodo.* An old hen makes good broth." Emilia happily abided by the old proverb whenever she thought that one of her charges had passed her prime. Within minutes, the poor bird found herself inside a casserole. Carrots and celery, onions, garlic, and plump little tomatoes sautéed in olive oil made the perfect bed of flavors and aromas to usher in the chicken's final culinary exploit.

❧ Pollo d'Emilia in Umido ❧
EMILIA'S QUICK CHICKEN STEW

How do we know when chicken is ready to eat? Well, Emilia would say to check the wing and if the meat comes away easily from the bone, the bird is done.

    1 medium yellow onion
    1 medium carrot
    3 cloves garlic
    ½ stalk celery
    ¼ cup extra-virgin olive oil
    2 tablespoons unsalted butter
    One 3½- to 4-pound chicken, cut into 8 pieces
    2 cups Emilia's Tomato Sauce (page 5)
    1 cup dry white wine
    Salt and freshly ground pepper *a piacere*
    Red pepper flakes (optional)

Peel and finely chop the onion, carrot, and garlic. Chop the celery. Sauté them in the olive oil and butter in a deep skillet over medium heat.

In the meantime, rinse and dry the chicken.

When the vegetables begin to soften, after about 5 minutes, add the chicken and tomato sauce. Cook over low heat for 15 minutes, then turn over the chicken pieces. Add the wine, salt and pepper, and red pepper, if using. Continue to cook for about another 30 minutes, or until the meat is tender and cooked through. Serve with crusty bread.

Makes 4 servings

There were puzzling chicken moments as well. Sometimes Emilia would abruptly grab a poor hen by the feet and swiftly immerse the bird in a big earthenware pot, *la conca*, filled with freezing water. No matter how much the hen protested, Emilia would continue to plunge her. "*Ma che fai?* What are you doing?" I'd ask in a surprised tone.

Emilia mumbled to the chicken without answering me. "*To', prendi questo, così impari, svergognata!* Here, take this and learn, you impudent thing!"

I eventually understood that the poor hen had just been in heat and that, in Emilia's eyes, this would distract her from laying eggs, the sole reason for her existence. The unfortunate animal, an unwitting victim of raging hormones, paid dearly for showing laziness in her daily productivity.

Once my brother and I received a magnificent gift from Nonna Valentina: a couple of "personal" hens. With some help from Emilia, I named mine *La Bersagliera* because of her glorious, warriorlike feather tuft that started immediately above her eyes and cut almost diagonally across her head. (The *bersaglieri* are a regiment well known—and sometimes mocked—for the multicolored feathers on their hats. When the soldiers run—and they seem always to be running behind a trumpeter—these feathers make a wonderful kaleidoscopic show of impetuosity and heroism.) We were allowed to take our hens out of their pen to play in front of the house, near the terrace. Both of them were perfectly tame and followed us everywhere, allowing us to touch their vermilion wattles and combs.

I loved the responsibility of feeding the chickens: First I had to go to the pantry, wherein lodged apples, potatoes, onions, garlic, all kinds of flour, sugar, and different varieties of pasta. In autumn, golden persimmons, picked unripe, were laid there in orderly rows, left to mature and slowly convert to glorious Pompeian ruddiness. On one shelf sat a big old pot that had seen better days, its sides slightly lopsided from several dents that registered a full life of usefulness. It would be filled with leftovers from various meals, and my duty was to add eggshells and bran flakes to make chicken feed. "Remember to crush the eggshells well, Patrizia, then mix them into the food, making sure that the hens don't notice," Emilia instructed me.

The shells, she informed me, added good calcium, but God forbid those astute hens should taste them. "*Sta attenta*. Chickens love eggshells," Emilia continued. "Unfortunately, once they've tasted them, they start eating their own eggs immediately after laying them." As our hens were the magnificent white Leghorn variety, the prized breed that chicken connoisseurs esteem for their egg production, this would have been rather unfortunate.

Afraid of such a frightful fate, I diligently crushed every single shell into minute bits and pieces. I added a little bit of water and, with a wooden spoon, stirred the concoction with great care until a gourmet meal was ready to be served to our pampered poultry. With much self-importance, I then trotted with Emilia to the henhouse, where I felt like Caesar in Rome, surrounded by all my adoring troops. *"Piro, piro, piro,"* Emilia and I cooed while ladling generous helpings of mush into their bowls, uttering the silly Italian onomatopoeic sounds that are supposed to captivate the poultry's curiosity.

One afternoon, I decided to conduct an experiment. It took me a long time to lure Paolo into my scheme, and even then he only joined in halfheartedly. "It's pretty simple, Paolo. I will just pour the leftover table wine from the glasses and we will serve it to the chickens," I told him brazenly. My brother reluctantly followed me to the end of the garden and watched while I spilled the looted wine into the chickens' water.

The bewildered look on their faces while savoring their new drink was worth all my travails. It was Hen Happy Hour, Tuscanstyle. One leg down, the other curled up, their dinky eyes discovering a new (and altered) world around them, the poor animals drank and drank, their voices eventually wandering off-key. They staggered all around the cage, until they just passed out cold on the ground.

By then, I was already regretting my little experiment and worrying about the consequences. I regretted it even more when my grandmother discovered it.

Nonna Valentina fumed. Emilia was petrified by the idea that her beloved hens would now stop producing their golden eggs. My mother couldn't believe that she had given birth to such a child. Fortunately—for the chickens and me—no casualties resulted from the poultry's bacchanal.

For my part, I had simply wanted to produce an instant Vov, the egg liqueur my mother favored.

Latte di Gallina
HEN'S MILK

This is an old Tuscan recipe, a good substitute for the liqueur Vov. Even now the name makes me giggle!

    1 large egg yolk
    2 tablespoons sugar
    1 cup milk, hot
    ½ cup Cognac or rum
    Nutmeg (optional)

Whisk together the egg yolk and sugar in a bowl, slowly adding the milk and liqueur. Add a pinch of nutmeg, if desired.

Makes 2 servings

In the Livorno garden, the rose reigned supreme, the undeniable queen of the grounds. A day would come, at the end of each May, when Nonna Valentina would urge Paolo and me to choose the prettiest rose of all, the Queen of May.

"*Bambini,* we will give *la più bella* the crown at the end of the day." This sent us into a frenzy of investigation, our quest inspired by the recent beauty contest fad. In the fifties, influenced by the American culture that had taken us all by storm, Italians launched the first Miss Italia contest. The entire population witnessed the fascinating new event. Grainy black-and-white television pictures and Movie-Tone newsreels brought the unfamiliar images into theaters, bars, restaurants, and homes. Everyone was enthralled by these native beauties parading their shapely legs and curvaceous bodies.

Forget about the dainty Queen of May! Paolo and I organized our own beauty pageant to bestow the great honor of Miss Giardino on the most beautiful rose of all. Armed with little notebooks, my brother and I approached our task like two pros. We carefully inspected the lusciously unfolded roses and checked the buds, predicting their future beauty and prospects. We selected, took notes, criticized, and finally voted. Nonna Valentina was the ultimate judge, and, as usual, handled her powerful position with the greatest fairness.

In the garden, we also made our personal toothpaste, courtesy of our clever grandmother. Several large bushes of sage and many varieties of mint and rosemary grew profusely near the chicken pen. On our way to feed the poultry one day, Nonna Valentina instructed us to pick some sage leaves with which to brush our teeth, in search of splendid whiteness. *"La salvia e' il miglior dentifricio naturale,"* she told us. It worked. The sage leaves' velvety texture and their wrinkles created the ideal friction over teeth and gums, cleaning the mouth and leaving behind a pleasant freshness.

At the end of our garden grew a small bush of *erba cedrina* (*verbena triphylla),* its silvery green leaves the perfect backdrop for its profusion of miniature lacy white flowers. Nonna would take us to the delicate shrub and teach us to rub our palms with a leaf to capture its fresh, unforgettable scent. The acute lemony verbena essence would enter the pores of our hands and linger deliciously for a long time. We had single-handedly invented the best of the Parisian perfumes right in our own backyard. Verbena had many other uses as well. Its leaves perfumed infusions, fruit salads, iced tea, and, once dried, homemade potpourri. It also contributed to the wondrous alchemy of Nonna's special beauty potion.

Every summer, my sister Giovanna and I waited anxiously for the Feast of San Giovanni, which occurred during the night hours between the twenty-first and the twenty-second of June, after the summer solstice. After dinner on the twenty-first, Nonna would lead us through the garden to gather as many petals as possible from geraniums, nasturtiums, freesias, roses, and verbena to make her magic elixir. "*Sarete bellissime!* If tomorrow morning you wash your face with this magic water, you will be beautiful."

Paolo, belonging to the male sex, looked on curiously from the living room door while I ran everywhere. I picked the farthest flowers on the highest branches of the magnolia tree—the closer to the sky, the purer they seemed—and I dropped on my knees to canvass the dark foliage in search of the best specimens among the lilies of the valley, the miniature bells the fairies loved to use as chimes for casting spells. I stretched to reach the tallest dahlias, painstakingly studying the different shades and the crispness of their elongated petals. When our baskets were full and the front pocket of our overalls overflowing with floral loot, I took Giovanna's little hand in mine and we ran to the terrace. Nonna filled a large silver bowl with water and then scattered the leaves and petals over its shimmering surface. Cinnabar-red geraniums floated as light as feathers, the tiny lilies of the valley joining them in an ethereal knot of red, white, and green. The *erba cedrina* sank slowly to the bottom along with the laurel leaves and the sporadically found white *zagara*, the orange tree flower.

Then it was time to let the bowl rest on the marble table overnight to absorb the magic early morning dew. "*Nonna, ma sei sicura?* Will it really work?" I eagerly asked, hoping for a positive answer, wishing to be reassured that beauty was just waiting to spread its charm over my features. "Will I shine like the splendid princesses from the fairy tales?"

I went to bed, counting the hours that separated me from morning. I never beat Nonna Valentina to an early start; she was always up first, perfectly dressed and ready to commence her day with her usual composure. But on this day, breakfast could wait. I ran to open the French doors and retrieve the silver bowl.

"*Non è cambiato niente!* Nothing has changed!" I exclaimed, seeing that the water still looked the same. Had the fairies really blessed it?

Giovanna and I waited for Nonna's sign and then splashed our faces with the magic water. Our hands came away with bright petals clinging to our nails and between our fingers; tiny leaves stuck to our cheeks. Rivulets trickled down our noses and lips, gently spilling over our nightgowns. We looked at each other in wonderment, our skin pleasantly chilled by the water in the cool early morning air.

"Is it working? *Nonna, siamo belle?* Are we beautiful?"

Tu Vo' Fa' l'Americano

Nonna Valentina, the author, and Zia Adriana

To Italians in the fifties, being—or acting—American was definitely cool, a distinctive virtue that would propel the lucky ones into the highest spheres of admiration. Songwriters and moviemakers recorded the phenomenon with loving humor, absolving the wannabes from their maudlin performances. In 1958, Renato Carosone, the famous Neapolitan musician, broke records with his popular hit *"Tu Vo' Fa' l'Americano,"* in which the hero, in his futile attempt to look American, drinks *wiskan-soda* but immediately feels sick. He wants to play *basuballa,* dance *rockanrolla,* and smoke *Camelle* cigarettes, but it is his mother's wallet that will ultimately pay for these extravagances. The refrain mirrors a popular reaction to the younger generations' use of the American language: How can anyone express his love in English under an Italian moon? How can "I love you" stand up to *"Ti amo"*?

A well-known Italian comedian, Alberto Sordi, capitalized on this widespread reaction, portraying it beautifully in one of his first and most famous movies, 1954's *Un Americano a Roma,* in which he plays Nando Moriconi, an unsophisticated but cunning young Roman from a blue-collar neighborhood. Obsessed with all that is American, he wears sneakers, chews gum, and earns great respect in his neighborhood because of his mastery of the English language. Even the simple act of sucking *le caramelle col buco,* the exotic LifeSavers the American troops had introduced into Italian life, gives Nando a sense of belonging to a culture he admires from afar.

Nando repeats an amusing refrain, a nonsensical amalgamation of English words, uttered with a pronounced American accent. "What'sAmericanHelloboy?!" he addresses friends and foes alike. Paolo and I caught this particular phrase from our uncle Pierluigi and employed it all the time, on our way to school and at home, displaying what we thought was a good deal of street knowledge.

In one of the best scenes in the movie, Nando decides to prepare an authentic American meal. In his family's modest kitchen he mumbles, "Americanfoodohyeah!" while sneering contemptuously at the lovingly prepared plate of *spaghetti al pomodoro* his mother has set in front of him. "Go away, *spaghetto! Chi te vole maccheroni?* Who wants you, macaroni?" he says as he produces a feast with the skills he has extrapolated from television programs and Hollywood movies. Before the horrified eyes of the Italian audience, he mixes *marmellata,* yogurt, mustard, and milk in the same way he blends unrelated English words. At the end, cheerfully applauded by many chauvinistic moviegoers, he gives up his fancy, inedible "Americanfood" and hungrily launches his fork into a plate of spaghetti.

My own first encounter with American food happened when I was seven or eight, aboard the *Forestall,* the great U.S. aircraft carrier, which had come to the port of Livorno. My lieutenant father had been invited on board and had generously decided to take me along. Given its tonnage and bulk, the warship could not be moored at a dock, and a fast launch took us to the middle of the bay. We boarded to the familiar sound of the whistles that greeted a visiting officer. An enormous elevator lifted us to the main deck.

"Papà, it's huge," I whispered, squeezing my father's hand as he led me into the officers' mess. I was used to the much smaller Italian warships, where I would saunter down the precipitous hatch ladders, sliding on the handrail, to reach the officers' quarters. Once inside this ship, however, I sat silently during the polite preliminaries exchanged between my father and his counterparts, all the while eyeing the immense pile of cakes laid out on a long table. They reminded me of the fluffy sponges the fishermen sold beside the sea all along the Livorno promenade.

A steward who must have noticed my greedy stares passed the huge tray around, kindly bending low in front of me. I admired the sweets in all their bright, airy yellowness, took a big piece into my hands, and bit into it.

Such disappointment! Not only did it look like a sponge, it felt like one in my mouth. It was surprisingly tasteless, no smell, no flavor. I immediately disliked it and shyly started toying with the slice (at the top of the list of Highly Forbidden Activities), concentrating on dividing it into minute pieces and scattering them into the faraway corners of the pockets of my blue coat. For once, Papà was fooled, as he was too involved in his conversation to pay much attention to me.

On the other hand, some American foods did earn approval in the via Roma household. During the late forties and well into the fifties the most anticipated moment in our family's calendar was the arrival of Zio Pierluigi, my youngest uncle, who worked at Camp Derby, the U.S. military base situated between Pisa and Livorno. Like all the employees, he was regularly allocated chocolate, cigarettes, coffee, and other luxuries as part of his fringe benefits. But, among those rarities, the most sought after item was *il pane bianco,* the white bread Italians had not seen in decades because of the war. The Italians called these long rectangular loaves *pane a cassetta* (box bread), much like the Pullman boxcars that gave the bread its name in America. What an incredible difference from *piccie,* the large round unsalted Italian loaves made from coarse grains! The white bread didn't appear at our table on a regular basis—supply and demand being highly unequal—but whenever it did, it brought joy. Everyone gathered to smell the fragrant square slices of that emblem of American culinary refinement. Not a crumb was wasted.

Topolino, the weekly magazine that entered our homes in the fifties, was the lighthearted Italian interpretation of Mickey

Mouse cartoons. Everyone, children and adults, loved the Walt Disney characters that filled our lives with knowledge about the American way of living: newspapers delivered in the morning by children, mailboxes, little houses with backyards and front lawns. American culture subtly infiltrated Europe. What the English had not been able to accomplish through centuries of visiting Italy, Americans put in motion by conquering our hearts with the everyday life of a mouse and his acolytes.

Topolino became a cult object, revered and often saved as a collector's item. Our Como cousins, who owned a superb library, had gone several steps further, binding every issue since the magazine first appeared in green leather stamped with gold letters. What a pleasure to climb the stepladder to reach books of every kind—novels, classical plays, French *romans,* and, not least, the *Topolino* series.

My generous aunt and uncle permitted me to choose any book on the shelves and read at the great mahogany table that stood in the middle of the room. But the best part of the deal was that I was also allowed to take books to my room. To me, this meant fabulous evenings where bedtime became just a word instead of an enforced measure. Knowing very well that my mother was spending her evening downstairs enjoying the company of her cousins and forgetting about her bookworm daughter, I would read into the forbidden hours of the night. I lost myself with *gusto* in the enjoyment of hundreds and hundreds of past issues, published when I was still a toddler. Unbeknownst to me, I also began to learn the English language.

"Gulp!" ballooned next to Mickey Mouse's mouth as he gobbled down his food. *"Goolp!"* Paolo and I enunciated, rolling our vowels with delight.

"Slurp!" exclaimed *Pippo* (Goofy), seated nearby *Topolino* as he ate his soup. *"Sloorp!"* we intoned, prolonging the U sound, stretching it into our best Italian rendering. "Sigh!" appeared next to a distressed *Topolina,* and we immediately knew that *"Seeg!"* meant that she was suffering from something *Topolino* had done. "Sob!"—so easy to pronounce—clearly expressed her sorrow. "Smack, slap, snort, sniff," and "grunt" crowded the pages, accompanying our heroes' adventures with an emotional soundtrack recorded in monosyllabic simplicity. My brother, my friends, and I began to intersperse our conversations with *"sneef, groont, sloorp, seeg,"* and *"goolp."*

"Seeg! I got such a bad grade at school today," I would complain to my best friend Susanna, guiltily examining the merciless red ink on my math test.

"What a fabulous cake, *sloorp!"* Paolo would yell at the sight of one of Emilia's marvelous productions. His favorite was the golden *ciambellone,* the ring-shaped egg, sugar, and flour cake to which a generous tablespoon of grated lemon zest added a distinctive tang. It was best enjoyed when accompanied by a cup of hot milk: the ultimate *merenda. Sloorp* and *goolp,* indeed.

None of us had the faintest idea that "slurp" involved the ill-mannered, severely forbidden loud sipping. Throughout my childhood, I always thought that the word merely projected keen culinary interest.

Il Ciambellone d'Emilia
EMILIA'S LEMON TEA CAKE

Emilia put two eggs (in the shell) on the old balance scale, in one of the shiny copper plates; on the other, she put the equivalent weight first of sugar, then butter, and finally flour. Each time, when both plates stayed level in the air, Emilia knew she had the right amounts. I still follow the same procedure, but those without a scale will have fine results using the quantities below. Sometimes, after the cake had cooled, Emilia would slice it in half and fill it with delicious jam.

> 8 tablespoons (1 stick) unsalted butter, at room
>   temperature
> ½ cup plus 2 tablespoons sugar
> 2 large eggs
> 1 cup flour
> 1½ tablespoons baking powder
> ¼ cup rum
> Finely grated zest of 1 lemon
> Juice of ½ lemon

Preheat the oven to 375°F. Butter a 9-inch Bundt pan and dust it with sugar and flour, tapping out the excess.

In a mixing bowl, beat the butter with ½ cup of the sugar. Stir in the eggs. Add the flour and the baking powder, mixing well. Add the rum and lemon zest.

Pour the batter into the prepared pan. The batter will only be about 1 inch deep in the pan, and this is normal; the *ciambellone* comes out best when baked as a thin cake. Bake for about 20 minutes, or until a toothpick inserted in the center comes out dry. Cool in the pan on a wire rack.

Meanwhile, increase the oven temperature to 400°F.

Stir together the remaining 2 tablespoons sugar with the lemon juice. Unmold the cake and put it right side up on a baking sheet. Brush the cake with the lemon mixture and

return it to the oven for 5 minutes, or until golden. Let cool
before serving.

Makes 6 servings

When I turned two, my grandmother started a big scrapbook,
which she nicknamed *Il Librone*. The large volume—measuring
twenty inches by fourteen and bound in Fabriano paper with its
characteristic antique floral design—sat on a shelf in our library.
The little flowers were red and green, the corners and spine of the
book a rich burgundy red, and the large heavy leaves bound by
golden strings woven through the book's spine. Its generous
pages were entirely filled with covers and pictures cut out from
The Saturday Evening Post, The Woman's Journal, The Rotarian,
and other American magazines from the late forties and early
fifties.

Norman Rockwell was our "artist-in-residence." He had the
sensational ability to draw the kinds of pictures that make you
think. His paintings taught me more about the United States than
a thousand books of history and geography could have. Rockwell's *The Plumbers* was one of my favorite covers. I was horrified
and enthralled by the sight of the two soot-covered workers happily spraying each other with the lady of the house's fancy
French perfume. Ostensibly repairing the bathroom, they invade
their client's pristine space, clearly mesmerized by the profusion
of creams and bottles, and their gleeful looks and great smiles
suggest that they are having a grand time.

"Nonna, what do you think the poor lady will do once she
sees what they have done?" I exclaimed, scrutinizing the details

of the workers' dirty boots on the white carpet. "Do you think they will be punished?"

In Livorno, I had never seen a plumber dressed like those two, who sported exotic denim overalls over portly bellies that disclosed a tendency toward generous eating and drinking. Nor had I ever seen such a frilly rug, or the kind of vanity table portrayed in the picture. Kidney bean–shaped, with a glass top and an abundant skirt made out of two or three layers of white mousseline, it was the most exquisite piece of furniture imaginable.

"Patrizia, look at that little dog with his fuchsia ribbon hiding behind the vanity table. Can you see? He must be terribly worried about the same thing as you. *Chi la fa l'aspetti!* They will surely be punished!" Nonna Valentina assured me, confirming my fears.

Through *Il Librone,* I grew up knowing all about banana splits and baseball mitts. I dreamed of sleeping in a great black American train, crossing from the East to the West Coast on Christmas Eve, waiting for Santa Claus to come. I fantasized of being in college and receiving a care package, courtesy of one of my other favorite illustrations, which shows a group of hungry freshmen applauding an enormous cake that has just made it to their dorm from the post office. The substantial treat is iced with a beautiful thick layer of white sugar glaze and decorated with candied red cherries. Who had sent the cake? A grandmother or a loving parent? A caring aunt or a doting godmother? After seeing that gorgeous pastry, who would ever want to eat Emilia's plain lemon cake? I desperately craved something as delicious looking as that angel food cake.

* * *

A big map of the world hung on the wall in my grandfather's library. I used to stand on tiptoe on the maroon leather armchair to study every detail with the utmost concentration. Framed in solid dark wood, the map was dotted with multicolored pins. Flaming red represented the countries my grandparents had visited many times. America, where Nonno and Nonna traveled twice a year, held the most red pins, proudly identifying New York, Washington, Evanston, Lake Placid, Miami, San Francisco, and many more familiar names.

"Do you know that our country, Italy, is smaller than most states in the USA?" my grandmother asked. I shook my head in amazement at such geographic magnitude. None of the other European countries heavily dotted in red seemed like much of a journey. Somehow they didn't count, since barely a few hours separated us from France or Switzerland, Germany or England.

Green pins marked places my grandparents wanted to visit but hadn't yet, like all those mysterious countries behind the Iron Curtain. My grandfather was a staunch anti-Communist, prone to forget his manners as soon as the conversation veered toward any possible interference of *quei porci* (those pigs) in the Italian government. *L'Unità*, the Communist daily paper, was considered the equivalent of Satan's official publication.

White was for the pins that dotted the nations about to become the next trip. I used to sigh and say, "Grandfather, I wish I could come with you!" and he invariably answered, "*Bimba*, you will visit this planet more than I ever will."

Though they were profoundly proud of being Italian and of being able to introduce our culture and traditions wherever they went, my grandparents loved belonging to the world, and not just to their own country. Nonno's import-export company required much traveling abroad, which he gladly combined with his social life. Once in a while, his friends reciprocated with visits to Livorno and descended on us bearing treasures.

And what treasures! For us, the starry-eyed grandchildren, they seemed the most incredible gifts we could wish for. Splendidly different, they always created a sensation among our peers. On a particularly lucky day, I received a booklet of paper dolls, which immediately became my claim to fame at school. The dolls were the actors Tony Curtis and his wife, Janet Lee.

Frankly, Paolo and I had no idea who they were, since television, movies, and magazines were largely forbidden to us, but I trusted the generous donors who had assured me that this was the most famous couple in the movie business. Both dolls owned splendid clothes and shoes, fancy hats, and unusual accessories. Tony's expansive wardrobe featured garish shirts and bow ties, while Janet obviously relished ownership of a truckload of skirts and shorts. The smile never abandoned her perfectly made up face, framed as it was by a precious helmet of stiff golden curls. Improbably high-heeled sandals accompanied fur coats (including a de rigueur white mink, of course) and sequined evening gowns. Tony's silk pajamas (who had ever heard of such extravagance?) were paired on the pages with Janet's lavishly laced nightgowns. I matched all that was available and luxuriated in the pleasure of transforming Janet into the beautiful star I had learned to admire. I thought she represented the epitome of elegance and sophistication. Cutting out the clothes and accessories and assembling all the different parts was enough for me to lose myself immediately in a paradise of imagination. Hollywood had landed in Livorno garden.

One day, courtesy of another munificent friend of my grandparents, Paolo and I became the proud owners of two wonderful Davy Crockett coonskin caps, complete with hanging tails. They had come directly from the Wild West, instantaneously generating cheer in the via Roma children's quarters. The only difficulty was the distressing problem of negotiating who was going to be Davy.

Fortunately, Paolo and I reached a Solomonic decision: we would both become the famous trapper. From that moment on, we filled the Livorno garden with jubilant calls. Imagination had flown us across the Atlantic Ocean, over the Rocky Mountains, and deep into the wonderful American West.

"Davy!" yelled Paolo, on horseback, exploring the immense plains of Wyoming.

"Yes, Davy?" I answered, wading through the Colorado River with my faithful horse Black Beauty, her name derived from another story my grandmother had read to me.

"Here I am, Davy!" shouted the courageous Ranger Paolo, directing his rifle at an immense grizzly bear to save an entire settler family from gruesome death.

My grandfather, Nonno GianPaolo, was very strict and highly opinionated on several subjects. Nonno had much to say against people who lived in indigent neighborhoods, lacking the most elementary comforts, but who nonetheless found the means to buy themselves expensive television sets. "*Guarda,* Valentina," he addressed my grandmother, shaking his head, "look at that forest of antennas on the roofs of the poorest buildings in Piazza Cavallotti!"

He was referring to the Piazza del Mercato, which was surrounded by the most poverty stricken houses in the city, still bearing scars from World War II bombings. The window shutters were falling apart and the many cracked windowpanes reflected heartbreaking misery. Enormous holes remained unfilled in the shelled facades. Yet, sure enough, hundreds of antennas tied to crumbling old chimneys crowded the skyline atop the ruined roofs. In one of our many allusions to classicism, television broadcasting was—and still is—often dubbed *dall'Etere*. The "ethereal" escape provided by TV had become the newest, most accessible entertainment for Italian families, an easy way to flee a depressing quotidian reality.

Beyond television, other major targets of Nonno's merciless wrath were the movie industry, Coca-Cola, and chewing gum. All were deemed particularly offensive because of their vulgar commonness. *Volgare* branded all that I really wanted to do or possess. I couldn't possibly understand why my family banned the best things life had to offer.

Movies were off-limits except for Walt Disney films; Hayley Mills, in her sweet Pollyanna fashion, was practically the only actor considered suitable for our innocent eyes. As an entertaining night out, *La Cavalleria Rusticana,* the famous opera by Mascagni, was about all I could hope for. As soon as one of my blue party dresses was extracted from my meager wardrobe, I knew that I was in for a long, culturally meaningful night with my grandparents. Fortunately, Nonna Valentina always chose operas that would appeal to a young child, so that after the initial resentment I would sit wide-eyed, witnessing the fascinating commotion on stage. As one would expect, *The Merry Widow,* with its extravagantly beautiful costumes and cancan scene, was by far my favorite.

I was surprised that the fabulous American people, so esteemed by my family, could survive those daily threats to their health—bubble gum and Coca-Cola, designed to destroy human intestines and bring entire populations to a quick and painful death. Chasing the forbidden treasures, I used to sneak out to the nearby bar a few doors to the left of our house. *Il barrino,* aptly named by my brother and me, was a tiny space with a counter and two tables where I knew I could find the magic *gomma Americana.* It was dispensed from freestanding transparent cylindrical containers, full of multicolored balls. What a great pleasure to introduce a few liras into the slot and to witness the little sphere's precipitous fall from the hole at the base of the machine. The gumballs rolled into my impatient hands and were quickly shoveled into my awaiting mouth. Propelled by my skillful blowing, the gluey substance metamorphosed into wonderful balloons, always ready to come crashing down over my nose and chin. I had been told horrifying tales about what chewing gum could do. "Continue to chew, and undoubtedly you will turn into a cow ready to be shown at local zoos. *Sembrerai uno scoiattolo!* You will forever look like a squirrel!" Mamma and Nonna forecasted gloomily. My cheeks would blow out of proportion, and no one would ever want to marry me. And if I inadvertently swallowed the gum, my bowels would glue together.

I didn't care. As the Italian saying goes, "*Fatta la legge trovato l'inganno.*" I would surely be the exception to the rule. I was not going to allow my family to deprive me of these exceptional life pleasures, and I found every possible excuse to go to *il barrino,* which, besides the gum, offered all I really wanted: a big black-and-white television. The owners, a gentle middle-aged husband and wife, *il signor e la signora* Ceccherini, kept a sympathetic eye on Paolo and me as we spent afternoons there watching *Rin-Tin-Tin, Lassie,* and *I Love Lucy,* our intellectual milestones.

Provided we had completed our homework, Paolo and I were allocated one hour only to extract as much gratification as possible from those televised adventures. During that hour I wasn't permitted to order Coca-Cola—my family's influence reaching well beyond the house walls—but I loved our native version, *la gazzosa,* a kind of sweet soda served in transparent bottles, each containing a little black glass sphere. A clever way to keep the gas from escaping? I remember stretching my arms on the table, holding the bottle between my hands, leaning my face as closely as possible to study the little ball trapped inside. The soda bubbled its way up the pot-bellied bottle, pushing the glass ball into a frenzied dance of pivoting, swerving, and pirouetting in and out of the elongated neck, finally erupting, slowly, in a beautiful lace of transparent burbles and droplets.

Rin-Tin-Tin and Lassie, my favorite stars, fed my ever-present desire for a dog. It was all too clear that my beloved "personal hen" could not perform any of the stunts I witnessed during my prolonged stays at *il barrino.* Could she ever jump from a running train to save me from a scalping by an infuriated Sioux? Yet my mother and grandparents had proclaimed that dogs were out of the question and would never be allowed into our household. Was the fact that they couldn't lay eggs a determining factor in this arbitrary decision? Cats and chickens remained my only options for pet ownership, so I made do with them, but they lacked the charisma and courage of the canine characters I admired so much.

I elected *I Love Lucy* as my favorite program. Lucy's eye-catching makeup, her adventures, and the big heart that always materialized in the opening credits of each episode captivated me. That heart and Lucy's mouth seemed linked by more than just shape; even in black-and-white, I knew they were both unmistakably red. And the neighbors, Fred and Ethel Mertz, who, invited or not, perpetually popped in and out of their Manhattan apartment, interacting all the time with Lucy and

Riccardo (as we Italians pronounced his name), represented one of the most fascinating aspects of the show to me.

In our household, rather rigid visiting rules meant that no one was simply allowed to arrive uninvited. Expected guests were usually shown into the *salottino delle visite,* the little parlor to the right of the entrance door. There they were entertained until the tea was finished and the cookie tray depleted. We grandchildren were sometimes summoned, well combed and properly dressed, to greet the visitors, displaying our best manners: I curtsied and Paolo kissed the ladies' hands.

No guest would ever wander into our kitchen, or climb the stairs to the other floors. Lucy and *Riccardo* were obviously much more open-minded than my family, and, watching their program as carefully as I did, I imagined opening my door to friendly neighbors.

"Would you be so kind as to give me a cup of sugar?" That phrase sounded so urbane, familiar and foreign at the same time.

Unfortunately, Paolo had an acutely annoying habit of feeling sick almost every time we settled in front of the screen. Maybe the fast-moving faded black-and-white images were too much for him to look at for a solid hour. Whenever I saw his eyes wandering, I heartily nudged him in the elbow, afraid he would loudly broadcast his discomfort. At first, the attentive *signora* Ceccherini would provide a soothing *camomilla* for my queasy brother and carefully monitor the results of her panacea. If the tea was unsuccessful, though, she would send us home at once, swiftly terminating my American adventures.

Nevertheless, although Paolo's stomachaches happened quite regularly, we never lost heart; once back at home, we created plenty of entertainment, sticking to our American theme. Whenever we could, we crawled under the big table—magically transformed into our garrison—in the *stanza degli armadi* (armoire room) on the third floor. There we played to our heart's content, with Rin-Tin-Tin and Lassie occasionally performing extraordinary acts of bravery. Our raccoon hats, naturally, added authenticity to every scene.

Paolo's *soldatini,* who represented the *Sudisti e Nordisti,* filled our afternoons with endless hours of dramatic battles. The tin soldier set came with an impressive wooden fort, as well as a great number of American Indians and their splendid Palomino horses. Too young to know anything about the Civil War, we simply gravitated to the uniforms, our patriotic allegiances in reality nothing more than fashion choices. I was a *Sudista* (I loved the big hat and the sage-gray uniform), while Paolo took pride in the sparkling gold buttons that graced the blue *Nordista* outfit. *"Muori Nordista!"* I yelled, imparting a lethal blow to my brother's soldier. In our fantasy world, *Nordisti, Sudisti,* and *Indiani* mixed in surprisingly relaxed style, taking turns at bravely fighting each other, often sharing the same fort and riding the same horses.

In 1955, my father's career took us very briefly to Augusta, a naval base in Sicily. The six short months we spent there when I was seven were a tremendous change from our well-organized life in the Livorno house. After a semester, it was clear that schools in Augusta were not as good as those in Tuscany, and so my mother, Paolo, and I went back home. Yet in those few months, I encountered another evil of American civilization.

One night my father and mother, having attended a party for visiting American officers and their spouses at the Officers' Club, returned to our tiny two-room apartment in the cramped navy guest-quarters building. The forced proximity allowed me to hear easily all that my parents said in their bedroom, and, unbeknownst to them, I accumulated vast knowledge on several diverse subjects. On that night, I discovered the truth about a new music labeled rock 'n' roll.

From my parents' description, it sounded like something absolutely satanic. Papà and Mamma described the distinctive peculiarities of this recent musical fad that apparently carried no melody at all.

"Did you hear that new singer, Bill Haley? His howling is as grotesque as the strident notes of his songs," my father said contemptuously.

But the worst was still to come. Not only had this offensive music been played, but some of the American officers and their wives had dared to dance to it. Loosened legs and limbs had been hurled up in the rarefied club air and the ladies' composure wiped out by all sorts of body swiveling and kick-ball changes. Furthermore, the swirling bias-cut skirts had revealed more than a real lady should ever show. The hit song "Rock Around the Clock" and all it represented had almost instantly become the new target of my parents' contempt. Rock 'n' roll swiftly joined gum, television, films, and Coca-Cola on the List.

What had particularly horrified my mother was not the unrefined dancing, but the foreigners—men and women alike—who exited the club in a state of perfect inebriation, staggering down the marble steps. Several Italian couples, witnessing the ignominy of the U.S. Military Police round-up, stared, shocked and silent.

"Adolfo," Mamma whispered to Papà in their not-so-private bedroom, "what a shame to be arrested in front of everyone. Did you see how the MP threw those poor people inside the jeep? They looked like broken puppets."

I could see her shaking her head, opening her eyes wide, trying to understand this bizarre reality. My Sicilian father, who revered his wife's decorum, quickly delivered a diatribe, censuring the poor American ladies. Deplorably, after a few unkind, hasty pronouncements on their behavior, Papà uttered his final judgment: *"Puttane!"*

In the cozy corner of my own room, then, I had learned a new noun and an interesting new concept that sent me the next morning directly to my parents' dictionary. Since first grade, I had known that such tomes were fabulous repositories of very useful information. I constantly consulted them in search of scatological entries.

"Peto: a gas emission, more or less noisy, from the intestine."

What a great definition! Sharing my findings regularly aroused laughing fits in my brother and our best friends. *"Patrizia! Un altra parolaccia, dai . . . , per favore!* Another bad word, please!"

The entry for *puttana* read: "a person who favors anyone, or loses her dignity by means of money or personal interest."

It was puzzling at best. Were the American ladies paid to dance?

HOUSEKEEPING

The via Roma house

Built like an ox and with the fiercely independent attitude that becomes all good Livornesi of every social level, Adelaide came to our house twice a week from Montenero, a lovely mountain village a few kilometers away. Montenero was blessed with a famous monastery and a tradition of breeding superlative laundresses. These women came to town daily to collect dirty sheets, towels, and tablecloths.

Adelaide arrived early in the morning, entering through the service door with a rolled-up white cloth in her arms. She adroitly spread the large spotless sheet on the floor in the main hall, just between the heavily inlaid box seat that held old newspapers and the round table in the center. Perched on the last step of the big staircase and comfortably leaning on the wooden balustrade, I witnessed her modus operandi with great interest. Adelaide was always in and out in a matter of seconds. The housemaid brought down the dirty laundry from the second floor and filled her well-delineated fabric boundary. As soon as the items accumulated in a large heap, Adelaide gathered the four corners of the sheet and efficiently knotted them together, shaking the bundle to distribute the weight evenly. She briskly carried it outside to the horse-drawn cart where her husband waited patiently, reining in his loudly snorting mare. *"Oh! Oh! Bada mariuolo! Sta'fermo.* Keep still, scoundrel," he yelled in his thick Tuscan accent. Effortlessly, he picked up the heavy bundle and sent it, in one precise toss, to join the many others on the cart.

No lists, no itemized entries, just steel-trap memories and extraordinary organizational skills helped these illiterate women to manage their business. Once in Montenero, Adelaide joined the other women and washed her entrusted linen in the plentiful mountain spring water. Their only tools were elbow grease, the big antique stone basins, and corrugated scrubbing boards worn down through millions of washings.

But many were the secrets for obtaining the immaculate whiteness that characterized their laundry. The women boiled the clothes with ashes, an ancient bleaching secret, and energetically rubbed the fabric with soaped stones. The process took several hours and an incredible disbursement of aerobic energy. Once successfully scrubbed, washed, and rinsed, the laundry was spread all over the great fields that covered the mountain slopes. In winter, the freezing *Libeccio,* the local northern wind, took care of the laundry, crystallizing wet sheets, tablecloths, and towels, gluing their corners together and curling their sides. During the good season—probably not less than nine months per year—the wash dried on the grass under the sun, gently brushed by the breeze, or hung on endless clotheslines that crossed the fields, zigzagging along the incline of the land. To sleep in fresh sheets perfumed by flowers and herbs helped more than a tisane to conciliate a good night's sleep. What satisfaction to bury my nose in the pillows, closing my eyes and luxuriating in the scents of lavender and sage, broomcorn, clover and sainfoin, sedge and vetch that awakened memories of country excursions.

Electrical appliances did not make their appearance into Italian life until well into the late fifties and the beginning of the sixties, the decade that witnessed my country's unprecedented economic boom. Having banished television, my family was nonetheless attracted by the notion of helpful domestic devices. I witnessed the arrival of the First Washing Machine, the First Refrigerator, and, light-years later, the First Dishwasher.

Before the arrival of the refrigerator, we had a *ghiacciaia,* an icebox. The sturdy rectangular box was built of beautiful rust-colored cherry, with a heavy door that made it resemble a safe. A strong iron bolt locked it, protecting its wealth of ice.

The delivery of the enormous slabs of ice was as intriguing as Adelaide's quick invasion of our hall. Once more, a horse-drawn cart stopped in front of the service door, this time to let a couple of heavyset men jump down. First they covered their shoulders with burlap sacks; next they lifted the big custom-cut slabs onto their backs and secured them with ropes. Finally, they covered the ice with another piece of burlap, reaching behind with their hands to hold everything together. Only then did they move into the house. Water dripped all the way from the street to the ice-box, leaving icy puddles along the narrow corridor that led to the pantry.

A most enticing activity for Paolo and me was to steal the fallen ice shavings, quickly filling our mouths with impromptu *gelato*. We incited each other to devour as much as possible, invariably ending up with an impossible pain lodged between our eyes. Taxing our foreheads' oversensitive nerves, pangs of pulsating misery shot through our faces, affecting eyes and teeth, temples and skull. Agony notwithstanding, we continued to relish our unhealthy habit. It must have been a vaccination of sorts. The slabs were transported by way of unprotected and unhygienic carts; only God knew their provenance.

Emilia never noticed us; she was always busy monitoring the men and making sure that they didn't invade her precious kitchen. "*Via, via! Con quei piedacci!* Off you go, with those dirty feet!"

La ghiacciaia was used mainly during the summer, since in winter it was perfectly easy to store foods and liquids right outside Emilia's kitchen. The temperature seldom went below freezing—thanks to the mitigating influence of the Tyrrhenian Sea—so nothing stored outside in the hermetically sealed containers ever froze, and it would keep well for several days.

The philosophy of pantry stocking also was different in those days. Except for dry goods, every item was bought fresh and consumed within hours. Meat, fish, cheese, and vegetables were purchased to match the day's menu, with quantities cleverly calculated not to exceed demand. In the event we did have extras after a meal, Emilia would figure out a way not to *utilizzare* but to *autorizzare* the food: our leftovers were not simply "utilized," but "authorized" into another satisfying meal. It often meant creative solutions for our light dinners, where a good *sformato*, a timbale produced with the leftover zucchini and string beans from lunch, would be set forth accompanied by the usual *minestrina*, a consommé with small pasta, and a spartan piece of cheese. Fruit always ended the via Roma meals, a most annoying custom since, as soon as I was allowed to sit at the adults' table, I also had to endure endless lessons in table manners, emphasizing correct Fork-and-Knife Management. Is there a seven-year-old who wishes to eat an apple employing laboriously proper precepts? The process of peeling fruit elegantly required too many fine motor skills. The end of the meal became a real nuisance.

For milk, we visited Maria, *la lattaia,* a wonderful fat lady who sat behind a marble counter in her store across the street from our house. Voluminous cylindrical metal canisters lined the wall behind her. She lifted the close-fitting top of one of the containers and ladled out the requested quantity, precisely filling the half- or one-liter jugs. As soon as I grew old enough to cross the street by myself, I was charged with the great responsibility of acquiring milk for the household. My ego puffed up shamelessly. I must have looked like a miniature turkey, spreading my tail and strutting my billowy feathers on the way to the store, self-confidence oozing from every pore. Barely able to reach the white counter, holding a few coins in my hands, I'd place my order. I was pleased with the speed of service, since, encumbered since birth by a most annoyingly overdeveloped olfactory sense, I loathed the sweetish smell that exuded from all that milk and cheese. Ashamed of my reaction and afraid of insulting Maria, I'd inconspicuously hide my nose in the sleeve of my sweater, safely inhaling the familiar scent of laundry soap and faint cologne. The strategy kept me from the humiliating prospect of throwing up in front of everyone.

Maria sold many other interesting items, including *cotognata*, the fabulous derivation of quince jam and my favorite recess-time *merenda* at school. In a tantalizing glass box on the counter, she kept dozens of tiny orange cubes covered with coarse sugar and wrapped in cellophane. Since it was easy to prepare, Emilia also made it regularly for our household. She simply cooked down the jam until it reached a firmer stage and then, once it had cooled, cut it with parallel crisscrossing lines. The rest was easy: the cubes were rolled in sugar and there it was, our mid-morning energy booster.

Cotognata
QUINCE PASTE

2 lemons
2 pounds quinces
Approximately 4 cups sugar, plus extra for rolling

Slice the lemons, skin and all. Put them in a big pot of water and bring to a boil. Add the quinces, lower the heat, and cook slowly until tender, about 45 minutes.

Drain the quinces, and discard the lemons. Peel and core the quinces, and push them through a sieve set over a bowl. Measure the strained pulp and add 1 cup of sugar for each cup of quince.

Scrape the mixture into a saucepan, bring to a boil over medium heat, and cook, stirring, for about 15 minutes, until thick. Pour into an 11 x 9-inch glass or ceramic dish, cover, and refrigerate for at least a week, or up to 1 month.

Cut into 1½-inch squares, and roll each piece in sugar.

Makes about 3½ dozen pieces

Although the pleasures of going to the market were indisputable, sometimes Emilia chose to stay home and receive deliveries. Her room was on the third floor, where my parents, my siblings, and I also slept. A corridor and a long wall separated her room from ours, but her windows conveniently overlooked via Roma so that she could observe all movements on the street. Not one to curb her curiosity, Emilia spent hours checking on the neighbors, vendors, and passersby. She abstained from her favorite pastime only for her customary after-lunch *siesta*. If the doorbell rang during her moments of repose, she stuck her face out from under the tilted window shutters and yelled with all the strength of her lungs: "*Chi è? 'Un c'è nessuno!* Who's there? Nobody's home!"

The ensuing conversations were carried on from the sidewalk to the third floor, with a great outpouring of decibels, in total violation of Nonna Valentina's dictates. "Emilia, how many times do I have to repeat that in an elegant household no one is allowed to yell?" Nonna would reiterate impatiently, almost every day. But to Emilia this was the most efficient way to handle such situations. Descending and then climbing three flights of stairs was not her favorite activity.

Sometimes, when a small item had to be delivered either from above (a forgotten house key) or from below (medicine or multi-colored crocheting thread), Emilia's hand emerged from underneath the green shutters. Holding a long rope, she slowly and skillfully lowered a basket against the wall, navigating the perils of pediments and windowsills, until it reached its destination. Mission accomplished, the basket returned successfully to the third-floor window.

I loved watching this ritual, admiring its ingenuity and craving to perform the spectacular act myself. It never happened. Children were not allowed to lean out of windows.

My grandparents' second-floor bedroom was spacious, comfortable, and, for a young child, full of attractions. Two tall windows overlooking the garden flooded the room with luminosity and a wonderful sense of serenity. I loved spending time there, joining Nonna Valentina in her domestic activities or simply standing next to her dressing table, watching her write notes and letters. She always kept a little bouquet of fresh flowers—freesias and roses when in season—next to a little bowl filled with *mentine,* the tiny multicolored sugar dots Nonno bought on Sundays.

My grandmother favored old-fashioned candied violets herself, and she always kept a pink cardboard box of them in her top right drawer, festooned with drawings of antique white lace. I had fallen in love with the candies' vibrant blueness and vaguely decadent flavor. To me they meant cotillions, elbow-length gloves lightly touching a gentleman's arm while waltzing, a rustling of white lace, tiny silver dance-card holders. I had been initiated into that world of bygone elegance by Nonna's captivating stories of fancy-dress balls and the beautiful nineteenth-century accessories she kept on her dressing table.

She allowed me to play with her mother's tiny, elaborately adorned instruments for corset and shoelace tying. The splendidly emblazoned comb that fit neatly into its thin container and the mesh silver purse she fastened to her sash were tangible remnants of a quasi-forgotten past. I sniffed the miniature perfume bottle, searching for vestiges of a long-evanesced scent.

I always wanted to help Nonna when, with Emilia, she made up the beds. Linens and blankets, stripped from the beds, were taken to the open window and hung there for several minutes to *prendere aria* (air out). There they lost their languorous night feel, reinvigorated by the scents of the garden and the intensity of the sun. *Aria* was Nonno's obsession; his bedroom windows stood open at all times and, during the colder months, rendered our poorly winterized house glacial.

Tightly enforced Rules of Creasing and Placement had to be respected. Folding the embroidered portion of the sheet that would overlap the blanket—according to Nonna's demanding specifications—was no simple job. To add confusion to an already complex task, my grandparents insisted upon different bed-making parameters. Nonna could fall asleep only if her top sheet and blanket reached just to her chest, while Nonno found rest impossible unless he was covered up to his nose.

I barely reached the mattresses. Trotting around them, I would admire the imposing headboards, huge examples of skilled carpentry embellished with a profusion of carved flowers, garlands, and fruits. Their large square mahogany feet protruded awkwardly from the cascading pleats of the claret-and-amber-striped brocade spreads.

I watched in fascination while Emilia's hands delicately touched the beautiful linen and Nonna cleverly doubled over the large pillows, tucking them inside the bedspread. I wanted to be part of that ritual and shyly extended my hand to soften a wrinkle, to smooth an unspotted crease, caressing the precious silk.

"Via, via! Il letto non si fa in tre!" exclaimed Emilia, horrified at my touch. She lived by the persistent Italian superstition that said if three people ever straightened a bed together, the youngest one would die. *"Di sicuro!* For sure!"

"Don't ever believe in those silly tales," my grandmother countered as soon as Emilia left the room.

I wasn't really sure whom to trust. Nonna was the repository of knowledge, of course, but what about Emilia, who had also taught me so much? If she said that I would die if I touched the bed, then maybe it was not a bad idea to keep at a safe distance.

So I looked reverently from a couple of meters at those imposing beds, contemplating the power they possessed. Death? One simply never knew . . .

We Italians have always invented extravagant superstitions, having obtained this expertise from our predecessors the Etruscans, the Latins, and the Romans. After all, those populations endlessly scrutinized the sky to observe flights of birds and movements of clouds in order to predict the future. They even killed lambs to discover the interesting prophesies and valuable information contained within their wretched offal; every event offered hidden meanings, as I had discovered in my history book. Numbers contained divinatory messages: *"Numero Deus impari gaudet,"* said Virgil. Jupiter loved uneven numbers.

Emilia had also often informed me that the numbers three (except in bed making) and seven were sure to bring great luck.

Here we were, centuries later, still jumping in horror if a black cat crossed our path, or if a hat or handbag was inadvertently left on a bed (unavoidable prompt loss of money) or if olive oil was spilled on the floor (certain calamity for the family). A saltshaker passed from hand to hand without first touching the table? A swift seven years of anguish. "*Ne di venere ne di marte ci si sposa e ne si parte!* One cannot marry or start a trip on a Friday or a Tuesday!" Thank God for garlic, though. Garlic was a *toccasana*, a panacea that cured all evil. We simply needed to keep some on our persona, Emilia said, and all would be fine.

Beyond Nonna's candied violets and the beds, my grandparents' room held many other wonders, the best one its frescoed ceiling. I loved to lie on the floor on the faded Persian rug, admiring the scene over my head. Aurora, complete with carriage and horses, and her famously pink fingers, drove away from the darkness of night, leaving behind clouds, moon, and stars, propelling her auspicious light into the world, heralded by rosy angels and caroling cherubs. "*Nonna, dai, raccontami la storia.* Tell me the story again, please. . . ."

Next to the beds stood two beautiful commodes, richly decorated in the same nineteenth-century style of inlaid and carved ornamental flora; inside, they hosted two chamber pots. This particular feature of my grandparents' secret life fascinated and puzzled me. My grandparents had two big bathrooms for themselves, an extravagant feature for those times. Nonno GianPaolo had built the state-of-the-art bathrooms complete with every modern accessory, elegant chrome faucets, and crystal shelves, a His and Hers seldom seen in the Italy of the fifties. Both opened up onto their bedroom. Why then the need for chamber pots?

The objects themselves were extremely beautiful, made of

white porcelain painted with roses, lilies of the valley, and daisies. Each sported a big handle that protruded from one side; they weighed a ton.

After my grandparents had dressed, while they enjoyed their breakfast in the downstairs dining room, Emilia and Concetta would empty the pots. I often sneaked in to watch the cleansing proceedings, intensely interested in investigating the rich amber liquid that filled them to capacity.

"*Dio mio!* They must have drunk lots of water last night," I'd tell myself.

Unfortunately, Mamma highly disapproved of this habit and as soon as my brother, Paolo, and I grew up, we were no longer allowed to use chamber pots. We had to cross the unlighted third-floor landing to reach our solitary bathroom. I was so scared by those nocturnal expeditions that I always tried to hold it until my kidneys hurt. My father's loud snoring thundered through the rooms, contributing to the terror of my brief missions.

Not only did Papà snore like the giants of fairy tales, he was a liar, and I had proof. He had cajoled me into eating fish by informing me that its phosphorus would make me glow. "*Mangia il pesce, Patrizia.* If you eat it, you are never going to need a flashlight. You will simply walk in the darkness and see everything."

It sounded so magical and heartwarming that I ate the disgusting boiled *merluzzo* and went to bed, night after night, convinced that sooner or later it would happen: my head would glow, and I would safely traverse the darkened hall, looking like a walking light bulb, dispersing wattage with every step. When it didn't happen, my huge disappointment prompted me to appeal to Nonna Valentina, confident that she would solve the impediments keeping me from incandescing. "Patrizia! Your father can never refrain from joking!" She laughed, lovingly caressing my nonphosphorescent head.

✤ *Merluzzo al Vapore* ✤
STEAMED COD

This is perfect served with boiled small potatoes and *Salmoriglio* (page 189), a simple sauce of extra-virgin olive oil, lemon, finely chopped parsley, and oregano.

> 4 skinless cod fillets (each about 4 ounces)
> Juice of 1 lemon
> Salt *a piacere*
> 2 tablespoons extra-virgin olive oil

Bring a couple of inches of water to a boil in a saucepan over medium heat. Put the cod fillets on a large heatproof plate, and sprinkle with the lemon juice and salt. Cover the plate loosely with a lid and place on top of the saucepan for 7 to 8 minutes, or until the fish flakes easily when poked with a fork.

Drizzle with the olive oil and serve immediately.

Makes 4 servings

"*Ogni cosa al suo posto ed un posto per ogni cosa.* A place for everything and everything in its place." The maxim helped us understand the principles of tidiness. In practical terms, it meant that at the end of each afternoon, at about six-thirty, Paolo and I put everything in order, collecting scattered toys and dolls, arranging them in their orderly places. Dolly and Maria Luisa, my favorite dolls, retired to their tiny beds; trains, cars, and boats parked and docked on wooden shelves.

"At night, all toys come to life," Nonna said with a serious look on her face. "If they wake up and find themselves scattered on the floor, away from their usual places, they will be terribly scared and won't be able to go back to their shelves," she explained to her stunned audience of two.

At midnight, it seemed, the electric train would set itself in motion, the dolls happily climbing aboard to enjoy a free ride around the rooms, exploring the floor, visiting the furthest recesses of the *stanza degli armadi*. The same adventures happened to the gray wooden horses and cuddly Teddy, to the brown dachshund on wheels, and to *Foca*, the stuffed seal my father had brought home from a trip.

If we didn't tidy up, we understood, a displacement syndrome would surely grow into a serious psychological problem for all of the toys. Obsessed with the idea, I couldn't sleep. A genuine paragon of untidiness, I found the thought that my dolls would wake up at night tossed around the floor, away from their habitual turf, terrifying. They wouldn't be able to keep their nocturnal friends company during the long, dark hours that stretched from sunset to dawn. My galloping imagination briefly turned me into a prototype of orderliness. For a while, I even tried to pick up bread crumbs that had fallen from our delicious afternoon *merende*. Bread crumbs, I reasoned, had the same right as toys to nighttime serenity.

At night, I sat up in bed, straining to recognize the muted steps, hoping to pick up the muffled sounds that would announce the toys' activities. Was it already midnight? Were the little *Sudisti* and *Nordisti* fighting each other without Paolo and me? I imagined my big doll Maria Luisa wishing to go for a ride and not being able to fit into Paolo's red model MG.

"Paolo, *sveglia!* Wake up! Do you see that shadow?"

"*Che ombra?* What shadow?" Paolo gasped, alarmed at having been jolted from his gentle dreams.

"*Si! La vedo, la vedo!* Yes, I see it! It's a monster, it's coming to eat you!" I couldn't accept that my brother slept, unaware of the toys' fate while I fretted over their well-being.

Invariably, after a couple of my solicitous, thoughtful warnings, a scream arose from the bed next to mine.

"*Mammaaaaaa!*"

Our combined shrieks reached the dining room two floors below, shattering the peace of the evening meal.

"*Ancora, Patrizia!*" an exasperated Nonna would exclaim. "What are we going to do with her?"

COSE ORRENDE

The author and her shadow

R*elata refero"* said Herodotus. I, too, am relating
hearsay. The following happened when I was barely one and had
just learned to walk, but I heard the story enough times to giggle
in anticipation every time my family recounted it.

On a beautiful spring afternoon, I was placidly playing on the sunny marble terrace immediately outside the living room. My mother sat on one of the green-striped garden chairs, knitting and chatting with my grandmother. Suddenly a bloodcurdling scream erupted from my mouth and I froze in a sculptural stance: my legs semi-parted as if about to take a step, my arms positioned as if ready to start a cross-country ski hike. The only active part of my body was my throat, relentlessly emitting piercing sounds, my little face distorted in absolute distress. Mamma and Nonna jumped up and ran to my rescue.

Everything looked perfectly normal. No blood, no strange animals climbing over my legs, no foreign body imbedded in my nostrils, no visible corporeal anomaly justified my histrionics.

Mamma took me in her arms. I looked at her, grinning with my best seraphic smile, and instantly stopped screaming. Only after a few minutes of reestablished calm, assured that everything was perfectly fine, did she put me down. One second later, my face once again crumpled in panic and I resumed the earsplitting yelling. What to do? My frightened young mother lifted me up anew and once more my face turned, in a nanosecond, from sheer terror to heavenly joy, like the Greek tragedy and comedy masks: the side of Happiness unexpectedly transforming into Despair with a clever twist of guise.

This sequence happened several more times, with both Mamma and Nonna increasingly baffled. "*Saranno le gambine?* Do you think something is wrong with her little legs?" asked my mother.

Finally Nonna solved the mystery: "*Ma è semplicemente l'ombra!*"

I had discovered my shadow, a concept too frightful to accept without fighting. The idea that my feet were connected to that black shape, that I would take a step and it would follow me, that I would turn and it would continue to stalk me, was terrifying. I could relax only in the safety of my family's arms, forgetting the dark monster, leaving it behind flattened against the marble tiles, lifeless without my terra firma presence.

The shadow was the first *cosa orrenda* of my childhood. More horrors were to come. The Removal of the Adenoids was one of the worst.

I had been taken to the doctor because I suffered from persistent colds. "Something must be done," agreed renowned specialist Professor Tinti, who, indeed, without delay, proceeded to carry out his mission. The ambulatory surgical lamp shone in a sinister way, reflecting off the white enamel basin's edge. Complete darkness surrounded this luminous spot, with me in the middle, enveloped. A couple of nurses kept my arms and body from moving. "*Ferma!* Be still, it will be over quickly."

Abruptly the doctor grabbed my head, pried open my mouth, and inserted a cold metal instrument that locked my jaws into a permanent yawn. He then swiftly inserted his fingers and a pair of forceps, scrambling rapidly up into my nose, and *plop!* curious bodily matters fell with a soft thud into the basin. "*Finito!*" he exclaimed.

The basin turned red with blood, cascading and splashing everywhere in the goriest fashion. My adenoids, guilty of one too many colds, had been removed without a drop of anesthesia. It was all over in a matter of seconds.

"Where were you?" I accused my mother.

"I am sorry," Mamma said sheepishly. "I waited outside. I just couldn't witness what was happening to you." She had fainted in the waiting room, powerless to prevent my suffering. Everyone had come to the rescue of my young and beautiful mother, pitying her ordeal.

The sudden removal of a part of my body was a shock that left me resentful and angry for life. Even if deemed unnecessary, those infected adenoids were mine and no one had asked my permission for such brutal invasion and plunder.

I repeatedly asked my mother, "Why?"

"*Perchè si.* Because that's the way it was."

Italian patients in the fifties were treated with generally accepted negligence. Bedside manner was an unknown concept. The great doctors dispensed their science from the height of their baronial altars and the recipients of their wisdom had to suffer, preferably in silence. Hippocrates must have whirled like a top in his ancient tomb.

Dentists were no better.

When I was five, I was taken to Dr. Keller, the Livorno society dentist. My grandmother and great-aunt Adriana, Nonno's sister, accompanied me to my first dental appointment, filling in for my mother, who was visiting Papà in one of his faraway posts. A tall, lanky woman, Zia Adriana had inherited the unfortunately protruding family chin. Having spent many years in Nairobi, Kenya, with her Italian consul husband, Zio Gege, she carried an aura of knowledgeability about the ways of the world. Sweet and helpful, Zia Adriana became Nonna Valentina's great friend. Together they took good care of the grandchildren's well-being.

Was my tooth wobbling? Was it rotten? No one explained. The pompous Dr. Keller simply brandished his pliers with a smug look on his face, obviously pleased with himself and his absolute power over an innocent child. He entered the room in a great hurry, wearing his authoritative white coat, and approached me. Understanding that nothing good could come from such an imperious march into such a scarily equipped examining room, I quickly slid from the chair, pushed away the enormous white drill, and ran straight into the ready arms of his nurse.

"Patrizia, dove vai? Where are you going? It is only going to take a minute," said Nonna and Zia Adriana, trying to soothe me. They obviously didn't understand that a minute was a lifetime.

Back to the chair I went, kicking and screaming. The huge pliers took care of the rest, and my tooth was quickly out.

Disgustingly bloody things arrived once a week from the butcher in a cardboard container. Often brains were laid on the kitchen table, red veins glistening shamelessly in the daylight. The slimy, wobbly, squishy mass had an unsettling way of sliding all over the cutting board as Emilia prepared it for cooking.

First, the brains were thrown into boiling water for a few minutes, then lifted out and placed on a large plate. A revolting fetor filled the kitchen and the pantry. *"Emilia, ma fa schifo!* How disgusting!" my brother and I declared. The smell itself was a terrible omen, heralding a most unpleasant lunch. The thin external skin peeled off easily and the millions of tiny capillaries that traversed the objects were discarded. One by one they went, unappealingly accumulating on the side of the plate. The spongy mass was then cut into pieces, rolled in flour, and fried with butter and a little bit of olive oil, finally seasoned with a couple of fragrant sage leaves from the garden. Paolo and I were thereupon supposed to eat the unfortunate combination of fried brain and boiled zucchini. Who had ever heard of such an unappetizing possibility? "May we eat something else?"

But Mamma loved *cervello fritto* and tried to convince us that it was extremely good for our health. *"Bambini,* it will make you very intelligent," she would say seriously. We had to ingest it, willing or not.

In my teens, I was the guest of friends in their beautiful castle in the Sicilian mountains, a few kilometers away from the Tyrrhenian Sea and its plentiful fish offerings. One day, a big plate of unidentifiable fried pancakes was passed around at lunchtime. Golden brown and smoothly textured, they looked innocuous, even appetizing, until I discovered that they were *frittelle di nunnate,* or *bianchetti* in Italian. *Nunnata* in Sicilian dialect means "unborn": I had just been offered barely hatched sardines! All of a sudden an image of those transparent larvae, with their quasi-formed eyes popping out, materialized in my mind. I had seen them in the fish market of Livorno and stared in fascination at their wiggling out the last sparks of life inside great barrels of ice. I had sworn I would never touch them, let alone ingest them.

Remembering my mother's teachings, I dug my fork inside the patties and started my usual swallowing-bad-food routine: a bit of the offending food, a morsel of bread, and a huge gulp of ice water to anesthetize the mouth. Somehow, I successfully cleaned my plate.

"Did you like it?" my friend's mother solicitously asked.

"Oh! It was exquisite!" I answered, buoyant at having overcome *le nunnate.* Ruthless lying was sometimes a necessary corollary to forced politeness.

"*Nicolino! Presto!* Patrizia would like some more," the good lady said, summoning her butler. Another full plate of semidead-half-alive fish fetuses appeared before me. Good manners are worthless.

My family held in high esteem several so-called healthy remedies. Things deemed useful at preserving our well-being were adopted with enthusiasm and dotingly administered. "*Fa bene alla salute*. It is good for your health" inauspiciously accompanied all that was revolting.

Chocolate had to be eaten only in moderation, but *olio di merluzzo* was prescribed once a day, another inexplicable mystery of adult reasoning.

The kitchen was the theater for our midday doses of cod liver oil. The huge dark gray marble sink was the stage, with Paolo and me unwillingly propped against it like puppets.

"*Apri la bocca!* Come on, open your mouth, it will just take a moment!" Mamma would say in her sweet but firm voice. Under her gentle appearance, she hid the same iron determination of the English nannies who had plagued her own childhood. She expected military obedience.

A putrid smell reached our nostrils at the first unscrewing of the bottle's cap, forecasting the foul fishy substance concealed inside. Flaxen yellow, almost solid, the "medicine" undulated in the spoon as it was slowly proffered to our firmly shut lips. After a lot of cajoling and pressing from Mamma and Nonna, the terrible liquid was finally swallowed.

Emilia looked on, curious to see how the daily drama would evolve. "*Po'rini!* Oh poor things! Here, eat a little bit of *cotognata*," Emilia offered, whispering encouraging words in her thick Livorno accent. The bright orange cubes of sugary pleasure were popped inside our mouths as soon as the medicine was administered. The wonderful treat represented nothing more than a palliative; our taste buds had been severely traumatized.

Oil acquired negative connotations in my childhood lexicon, especially when coupled with castor. I had always suffered from digestion problems and my *mal di pancia* was famous in our household. My tummyaches came with an accompanying high fever that would keep me in bed for a couple of days. Zia Adriana knew what to do: *olio di ricino,* extracted from the seeds of a tropical plant, was the sure remedy. My helpful *zia,* with her unending kindness, provided the stuff readily prepared by Dr. Roncucci at the Farmacia dell'Attias, a block away from our home.

Though I had developed a theory that constipation was preferable to *olio di ricino,* the family never ratified my precocious scientific breakthrough. The oil's overpowering smell even caused my mother to look sicker than me, the unhappy recipient of the salubrious therapy. *"Mamma, ma pensi davvero che sia commestibile?* Do you really think it is edible?" my mother asked Nonna Valentina.

Demonstrations of family love generally followed the forced ingestion of these repugnant remedies. Nonna exhibited her usual cleverness by showing me the *Librone* page that illustrated my ordeal exactly. The artist, Hugues, had painted a child in bed, holding the blankets up to his nose to cover his tightly shut mouth. The doctor has evidently prescribed a dreadful medicine, and both parents are trying to feed their son a spoonful. The mother beguiles him with eager cheerfulness: "Take the medicine, it is good! Look at him!" pointing to the unfortunate father, who, in the name of good parenting, is swallowing the syrup himself and pretending to enjoy its taste. The fingers of his left hand are stretched behind his back in agony.

I felt relieved. After all, those American children had something in common with me. Granted, they had television, Coca-Cola, and chewing gum, but they too had to succumb to the brute force of doctors, dentists, and parents. Despicable syrups were thrown down their throats even in that civilized, faraway country.

Whenever the flu struck, a new *cosa orrenda* materialized to torment us. My family believed that frequent bed changing was essential to restoring good health. Emilia and Mamma would envelop the ailing child in a heavy blanket and temporarily deposit their charge in a nearby armchair. Windows were opened wide, regardless of the season. The magic fresh air supposedly killed all kinds of germs. But what a great relief and pleasure to crawl back into the fresh, crisp, ironed sheets, drifting in and out of sleep, my cheeks happily burning with fever while another efficacious cure was being prepared.

If congestion reached a dangerous level, Mamma, followed by Nonna Valentina, would suddenly appear carrying a steamy cloth in her hands. This condition called for *impacchi di semi di lino,* nauseating hot linseed compresses. The health-promoting concoction had to be mixed outside Emilia's kitchen, as the smell was too intense to be allowed inside the house. The seeds brewed for a long time on a portable gas stove, continuously stirred with a special wooden spoon. Finally, the mush was bundled up in layers of cotton rags cut from old bedsheets. The last wrap was made from a piece of woolen fabric, designed to ensure good thermal insulation.

Mamma would open my cotton nightgown just a couple of buttons under my chin, at the level of my lungs, and tenderly apply her miraculous contrivance. It weighed a ton and instantaneously toasted my delicate skin, all the while emitting its terrible fumes. It wasn't easy to lie still and hold the scalding poultice in place. It tended to slip, transporting the gown's fabric with it. I felt quasi-strangled and oppressed by the combination of weight, heat, and stench.

"*Brucia!* It stings!" I whined.

"*Puzza!* It smells!" I protested in vain.

"*Fa bene alla salute.*" Mamma would sit next to my bed, firmly holding the compress in place, ignoring my complaints.

A few years later Italy started marketing a brilliant American invention, Vicks VapoRub—*Veex Vaporoob,* as we proudly pronounced it. Suddenly the outlook for congested chests had never seemed brighter; the eucalyptus and mint vapors that shook our nostrils and brought tears to our eyes were a welcome evolution from those *semi di lino* nights.

Nonna Valentina often chose to entertain me in my poultice-afflicted hours. She sat next to my bed and read in French from my favorite authors' books. Never for a second did I suspect that these famous writers had composed their books in English; my grandmother, for once, had forgotten to explain a detail. For all I was concerned, Agatà Cristì—who, after all, had given the world the famous detective Monsieur Poirot—was as Gallic as they came! I eagerly listened to Nonna's rendering of those wonderful "French" adventures, *Les Cinq Petits Cochons,* also by Agatha Christie, *Les Cinq Pepins d'Orange,* by Arthur Conan Doyle, and many others.

Among the many memorable readings of those early years, one stood out for inciting daunting, recurrent nightmares: *Struwwelpeter (Slovenly Peter).* My father liked to translate, slowly, into Italian for us from the dog-eared original German edition of his favorite book. The brightly colored cover showed a child with long hair and untrimmed nails so long they curled at the ends. In Italian, the title conveniently became *Pierino Porcospino (Peter Porcupine)* to emphasize the unkempt looks of this boy who regularly refused to bathe.

In one scene, a hair-raising tailor jumps out of a door, brandishing a giant pair of scissors. With two deadly strides of his long legs, he reaches the young Conrad and abruptly cuts off the child's fingers. "But, Papà, Conrad was only guilty of sucking his thumb!" I screamed. The tailor's terrifying appearance brought shivers to my spine and simultaneously produced unsettling hydraulic consequences. At the arrival of the bloodthirsty tailor, I always had to run to the bathroom.

Papà, who enjoyed the tailor tremendously, nevertheless finally turned the page so we could face Augustus, the kid who would not eat. Day after day he wastes away, refusing to swallow his soup. His body becomes thinner and thinner, until he looks like a shadow of his past self and dies. Grinning, Papà added his personal touch to the scary tale: Augustus's parents chose a soup tureen as their child's tombstone.

I was unequivocally convinced that the *minestrone* had been the culprit. "*Vedi, Mamma?* Who knows what will happen if you insist on feeding me *minestrone?* Maybe I will die too." I boldly tried to use those nightmarish stories to gain useful points with my mother. Success eluded me, and once a week *minestrone* continued to appear in my bowl.

My absolutely favorite horror story concerned the revolting habits of Papà's Sicilian cook from his childhood. "*Dai, Papà!* Please tell me again about Donna Micia and her celebrated *polpette!*" The story's lurid details would flow freely from his lips, almost at my first plea. My reaction never disappointed him.

"When I was a child, maybe six or seven," my father would start, "I used to sneak out of the house into the garden to peep through the kitchen windows. In those days, children were not allowed to spend time with the help, but I was fascinated by what I had discovered and never reported to my parents."

At this point, I would settle even more comfortably in my chair, sinking with pleasure into a delicious quiver of anticipated disgust, knowing that the stomach-turning details were about to be delivered.

Nonno Federico, well known for his bizarre habits, wanted his dinners served in the garden without exception at 6:30 P.M., electing to eat certain dishes and only certain dishes. Eating in the bright, hot, early evening hours was a disaster in quasi-tropical Sicily, especially in the summer, but my goodnatured grandmother obliged, fanning herself in her formal evening gowns under the sweltering sun. Donna Micia's meatballs were Nonno's favorite recipe, and he raved about them to his family and friends.

These *polpette* indeed had a special taste. Was the cook using some secret ingredients? Rare herbs, a special spice? They had a salty tanginess he had never encountered before. One day, my father happened to pass in front of the kitchen windows and witnessed the unthinkable, unmentionable truth. "I happened to observe the most horrifying sight. I stood frozen, hypnotized like a mouse in front of a python!" After a clever pause, knowing perfectly well that I knew the story and just wanted to hear it again and again to delight in the euphoria of being shocked, he would ask, "What do you think I saw?"

"Please, Papà, please continue!" I begged.

"I saw big, dark, hairy Donna Micia, wearing her usual ample black skirt and a sleeveless top. It was summer and as usual Sicily was scorchingly hot, not a *filo d'aria* was circulating in the huge kitchen. Donna Micia sweated profusely while rolling the little *polpettine* in her thick hands, shaping them with her expert fingers. After shaping each *polpetta* into a perfect roll, before coating it in flour and dropping it into the frying pan, she would quickly pass it under her hairy armpits, where it picked up the pearls of her summer labor."

At the image of these dewdrops from the cook's bushy armpits transforming my grandfather's daily *polpettine* into gourmet food, I routinely shrieked and produced every available sound, expressing my satisfaction at having been once again successfully nauseated. My father would smile and look his usual cool self.

Donna Micia was the subject of another anecdote, in which her voluminous black cotton skirt played a rich role. She was exceptionally corpulent. Moving slowly and cautiously, she sailed like a galleon through doors and along floors, preferring never to leave her kingdom, the kitchen. But sometimes she would climb the few steps that separated the pantry from the back garden and sneak out, away from inquisitive eyes—or so she thought. My father described in meticulous detail her slow inching toward a grass patch and her abrupt stopping under the great carob tree. From his hideout behind the zibibbo grapevines that ran the length of the northeast wall of the house, he enjoyed an unobstructed panorama.

"Donna Micia walked to the back door, exhaustion already showing in the intense breathing that erupted from her capacious chest, accompanying her progress through the dark corridor. She ambled across the gravel path to reach the pleasant shade of the tree and calmly stood, feet apart. A look of concentration briefly passed over her face, followed by a triumphant smile and the eventual resumption of her walk. She diligently shook her capacious skirt, the convenient screen of her crime, and shuffled back to her work post in the kitchen. A large yellow puddle, delivered to Mother Earth with the same indifference as a wild creature in the woods, scintillated under the sun's rays."

Mamma had a celluloid doll, Maria Luisa, an extravagant gift that had been ordered for her in the twenties. Her complexion was an unnatural chalky pink and her features were quite ugly, with prominent cheeks and a huge forehead. A chubby chin surmounted by a small snub nose—together with a tiny rosy mouth—completed her perfectly rotund face. Her painted cerulean eyes were in a perpetually surprised stare. Her hair, naively drawn in singular lines precisely traced on her big head, ended in a tidily arranged forelock that framed her brow. Quite big, reaching a height of about twenty-seven inches, she, and her beautiful wardrobe, had surprisingly survived the war years. No one had found her in the nursery rooms on the third floor. Had my grandmother stowed her away in a secret place? Maybe Maria Luisa's stolid face hadn't appealed to any of the intruding soldiers. In any event, the doll ended up in my caring hands.

I loved Maria Luisa with all my might because she represented the special world of my mother's childhood. She symbolized a precious link to a time when I had not existed; I treated her with the utmost respect.

I enjoyed changing Maria Luisa's dresses, reverently touching the old lace garments and the knitted caps that tied under her chin with shiny silk ribbons. Her chubby legs were covered with fine white stockings that ended in soft leather shoes more like laced-up white slippers. One afternoon as I played in the garden in front of the open living room doors, it occurred to me that I had forgotten Maria Luisa somewhere upstairs in Nonna's quarters. I looked up to see my grandmother appear at her window on the second floor.

"Nonna! Maria Luisa is in your room. I am coming to pick her up," I said, moving toward the house.

"*Aspetta!* I will send her down with a special elevator," Nonna replied with a wink.

With that, she proceeded to tie the doll in a sling of ropes, dexterously harnessing torso, arms, and legs. Nonna leaned out her window and started sending Maria Luisa down the wall of the house. The doll had to surmount a couple of pediments and cornices, but after those, her course seemed finally clear. Slowly, slowly, under my apprehensive stare, the doll continued her descent toward the safety of my waiting arms.

Suddenly the ropes simply came loose and Maria Luisa came crashing down, smashing her fragile face against the marble terrace. My poor grandmother, clearly guilty of dollycide, desperately tried to console me, suggesting that Maria Luisa would be sent immediately to the Doll Hospital to undergo restorative surgery. As usual, Nonna's words calmed me. She always knew best and I expected that she would never fool me with unreal expectations. The doll was quickly shipped to some mysterious place and, after weeks of my constant inquiries, she came back.

Thankfully, Maria Luisa's celluloid essence made healing her terrible injuries possible. Apparently a special tool, not so different from a foundry torch, had been used; its efficiently directed flame had fused together the broken pieces. A little bit of paint, and Maria Luisa was sent back home to enjoy the unwavering love of her family. The scars that quite prominently zigzagged her face held no importance for me; she was back, and that was what counted. I lovingly touched her face, caressing the corrugated celluloid, lightly fingering the coalesced seams of her wounds.

A similarly dark moment befell Dolly, my other favorite doll. Her name, which in English doesn't sound so original, represented for me the epitome of international sophistication. None of my friends had access to this kind of English verbal elegance. Dolly's exotic name spoke volumes about my acquaintance with the great American way of life.

Bought in the States by my grandparents, Dolly was soft and smooth, limbs resembling the real skin of a child. I loved to squeeze her soft belly against my body, comparing her with the stiff dolls that were available in my city. Nonna and Mamma knitted elegant clothes for her and I spent my time changing her outfits that included many embroidered shirts and several pairs of sophisticated tiny socks and shoes.

One afternoon, after completing some errands with Emilia, I came back home and ran upstairs to play with Dolly. Setting foot in the third-floor corridor that led to my bedroom, I arrived just in time to witness Paolo and his accomplice, Riccardo, jump up guiltily. They froze in silence and then hurriedly ran away.

Dolly lay on the floor, a pair of red scissors next to her body. Her fingers had been neatly cut off, their little tips scattered around, and a strange fine synthetic dust streamed from her open wounds, like white blood gushing across the floor.

"Che avete mai fatto? What did you do to my baby?" I wept, kneeling next to my doll. The pain, coupled with the still-fresh memory of Maria Luisa's accident, was too much to tolerate. Assessing the irreparable damage inflicted on my child, I resolved never to play with dolls again—they represented too much of an emotionally charged commitment.

But the most horrendous of all *cose orrende* was The Secret.

Tata Rina was the wife of Gino, one of my grandfather's employees at the office. Quite short and robustly rotund, she shuffled around her house wearing a pair of slippers made out of floor-polishing rags, a practical way of keeping her tiles as sparkling as diamonds.

She and her house both fascinated and horrified me. Always torn between wanting to visit her and immediately wishing to run away from the hypnotizing revulsion I felt once I stepped inside her rooms, I nevertheless managed to visit her a couple of times a week. Like a moth drawn to light, I had to have my dose of Tata Rina's bewitching lure.

She lived on the ground floor of a miniature house, directly behind via Roma. It took me only a couple of minutes to cross our garden and exit from the garage onto via Cecconi, quickly walking toward Tata's entrance door. Obsessively clean and orderly, she scrubbed every imaginable surface in her house daily with Varichina and Vim, the Italian equivalents of Clorox and Ajax. The bleach smell ambushed me as soon as she opened the door, grinning and welcoming me with exuberant kisses and hugs. The overpowering bleach stench, mixed with the sweet scent of cheap perfume, pervaded the house, gathering in corners, clinging to curtains and rugs. As soon as I walked in, I would immediately take possession of her rag slippers. I enjoyed gliding and artfully skating on the smooth floor wearing those clever inventions, outlining figure eights and performing complicated arabesques.

Apparently I was such a welcome distraction from her endless routine of scrubbing, washing, and cleaning that she looked forward to my regular calls, always preparing biscuits and treats designed to appease a child's perpetual appetite.

There were two primary attractions at Tata Rina's house.

First, she had an extraordinary collection of *uova di Pasqua*, the chocolate Easter eggs of Italian tradition. At Eastertime, every bar and store in Italy unveils these products of cheerful ingenuity, embellished with gaudy cellophane tissues, garish decorations of flowers, and multicolored ribbons. Each *pasticceria* establishes serious contests, sells tickets, and demands precise answers to difficult riddles. The eventual prize is a gargantuan *uovo di Pasqua*, weighing over a hundred pounds, that stands on the counter during the forty days of Lent. In the morning, between a *caffè ristretto* and a *cappuccino,* the clients discuss its extraordinary size and happily acquire the raffle tickets.

"Never seen such a big egg before!" they will exclaim admiringly, under the self-congratulating approval of the pastry shop owner.

Tata Rina owned hundreds of Easter eggs. She kept them untouched from year to year, Easter to Easter. Small, big, wrapped, unwrapped, decorated with sugar flowers, pastel chicks, spring leaves—they were displayed all around her living room. They stood on the floor, balanced on their multicolored plastic bases that resembled coffee-shop cups. They graced tables, counters, shelves, and windowsills. The chocolate smell transpired through the wrappings and the ribbons, permeating the room in sorry combination with the Clorox-imbued mops and rags.

The second attraction was the most fascinating, but also the most macabre.

"Please, Tata, could we go to your room?" I would ask after the first few minutes of polite conversation had expired and full visiting etiquette had been observed. In my impatience, I was prone to exhausting all preliminary niceties quickly.

"Andiamo, andiamo." Tata Rina immediately complied and stood up, happily holding my hand and taking me into her bedroom.

It was dark, with all the shutters tightly closed and the heavy satin curtains drawn. A lamp made of infinitesimal beads shone a faint yellow light on an imposing chest of drawers. An ornate mahogany framed mirror stood on its top, supported by several miniature columns that opened up into bizarre little drawers. Glass candle holders, Chinese lacquered boxes featuring languid maidens, tin containers decorated with beribboned poodles, and one gold-filigree Venetian *gondola* crowded the space.

In the middle of this *armamentaria,* close to the mirror and next to a colorful plaster Madonna and a doleful-looking wooden Christ figure, stood a big transparent jar covered by a square of precious white lace. Inside, swimming in formaldehyde, was her stillborn child.

That shrouded vase exercised a fierce magnetic pull. I always anticipated the moment when Tata Rina, conspiratorially, would invite me to examine her baby by briefly lifting the cloth while lovingly dusting the glass with a feather brush. The pinkish, quasi-jellied "thing" inside always sent thrills down my spine.

"Buongiorno, amore mio! Here, here is your mom taking good care of you," Tata Rina would whisper sweetly. *"Dormi bene.* Sleep tight," she would murmur to the jar.

Deciding that she had lifted the lace for an insufficient amount of time, I would engage her in meaningful conversation so I could study the jar. I needed to concentrate longer, to focus on its rosy floating contents, by far the most intriguing element I had encountered in my young life.

These afternoon sessions left me, for once, without words. With whom could I share this stomach-turning secret? I felt that not even Nonna, my enlightened and modern grandmother, could appreciate my fascination with fetus watching. I certainly never told my mother, for fear of not being allowed to continue my weekly visits. I prudently kept Tata's strange secret to myself.

One day, though, something happened and life suddenly changed. Maybe I had carelessly let a word slip, or Nonna's early arrival to pick me up had interrupted one of the hushed unveilings.

"You will not visit Tata Rina anymore," I was coldly informed.

"Ma perchè, Mamma?"

"Perchè no."

La Mia Famiglia Siciliana

Papà and Nonna Giovanna in Ganzirri, Sicily

My father's family arrived in Sicily, via Sweden and Germany, during the first half of the 1800s. Wealthy and well connected, they soon took a prominent place in life in the town of Messina, contributing generously to the community, giving to charity, adding to the intellectual and social life of the city. Later on, however, at the end of the century, they worked hard on the annihilation of the family fortune, spending and gambling without restraint. But the worst was still to happen. In the early morning of December 28, 1908, a terrible earthquake, which took 84,000 lives, gave the final blow to our family. Everyone except my grandfather—who was away at college—was killed, and the splendid Grill house that had occupied the major part of the waterfront was destroyed.

All was lost but the Grills' peculiar sense of humor. My father was a great raconteur, a storyteller of the first rank. He enjoyed talking about his childhood, his family, and the weird episodes that had dotted the intense social life of Messina, the ancient city on the Sicilian Straits. I loved listening to my father's chronicles of his impoverished but class-conscious childhood, the contrast between his family's old social rank and the new reality of their life.

My eccentric grandfather, Federico Grill, lived two distinct lives. In one, he remained the aristocratic gentleman who held a prominent place in his city's social circles; in the other, he suffered the humiliation of a daily job that didn't pay much and kept him in a subordinate position. Grandeur past, he had retired to what had been just one of the family country houses, Contesse. Still, he and his wife, Giovanna, continued to be invited to all the fancy parties, to which, in order to save money, he simply elected to travel by streetcar. His loving and patient young wife, in full regalia, adorned with jewels, thought nothing of lifting the hem of her long evening gown to climb the steps of the tram and holding on to the straps. Nonno Federico was also known for bicycling to his club, *Circolo dei Nobili,* to attend its formal dinners. He easily dismissed any sarcastic comment about his adaptive strategy of pinning together the tails of his white tie with a couple of laundry pins.

My father's tales ranged over many fields and social levels, funny and improbable stories that had kept the aristocratic beau monde of his city abuzz with succulent gossip. We children laughed, sometimes sotto voce when these tales were directed at his guests. He held forth in the living room, indulging friends, visitors, and family with his often-objectionable, highly entertaining stories. I would listen and store information in my memory while pretending to be invisible. Only my lashes would rapidly flutter off time, giving away my profound interest in the startling details I had just heard.

My favorite story was about a lady who had, in the thirties, climbed Messina's social ladder courtesy of the many millions her husband had recently accumulated. She was understandably anxious to impress the aristocratic families who still dominated the city's social life. What could be better than to erect a splendid mansion, complete with the latest technological advances? Having installed brand-new radiators in her bedroom, she proudly broadcast her newfound sophistication in sleeping *"con un gladiatore davanti e uno dietro,* with a gladiator in front and another one in the back"!

Contesse, the household where my father grew up, had miraculously remained mostly intact during the catastrophic earthquake. It had a big garden and a special pavilion called the *caféhaus,* in homage to the family's Germanic roots. The *caféhaus* was a celebrated example of eighteenth-century architecture, probably designed by the famous Carlo Falconieri. There the elegant gentlemen guests would gather after meals to smoke their cigars without annoying the ladies.

As a child, Papà wanted to run around the little village like a local street urchin, but his mother kept him under control. He both envied and resented the other boys' activities, able to admire their escapades only from afar. His great narration of *il trucco del limone* showed how he longed to be among the mischievous perpetrators of village pranks. On Sundays and on Patron Feast days, the local band would gather in the gazebo in the center of town. One day, when the musicians took their seats, a bunch of kids gathered directly in front of them, feigning great reverence for the men in their splendid white and gold uniforms. Was this fervor directed at the wonderful military marches the band was about to play? Or the popular arias listed in the day's program? The true motivation became clear when this group of fans extracted gorgeous, freshly picked lemons from their pockets and proceeded to bite into them with gusto. Simply watching them suck on the juicy yellow fruits generated a lot of saliva in the mouths of the trumpeters and the other brass players. False, strident notes immediately arose from the instruments, ruining melodies, to the endless pleasure of the naughty pack. At this point, the bandleader protested, shouting and chasing away the culprits amid the endless laughter of the irreverent crowd.

Unfortunately, none of the exciting events so well described by my father ever seemed to happen to me, but my own experiences and adventures taught me how the Sicilian branch of my family was definitely different from the Tuscan.

Messina was a relatively calm city, almost free of the Mafia influence that had strangled many other Sicilian places. "Messina is nicknamed *la provincia babba*," my father told us. "You know, *babba* in Sicilian means 'stupid,' and Messina has earned this name because *la Mafia,* for some inexplicable reason, has never settled in the city.

"Consider the fact," he went on, "that belonging to *la onorata società*—a euphemistic definition—could be a sign of distinction

in many poor villages and boroughs, since the Mafia was origi-
nally started to protect the less fortunate from the vexations of
the rich aristocratic families. It was considered smart to be able to
rebel against injustice."

Coming from Tuscany, where *babbo* means *"papà,"* I was
shocked by this definition. From then on, I satisfactorily
employed it every time I was furious at my father for imposing
some unwanted disciplinary rule, muttering, *"Babbo, babbo,
babbo."*

We went to Messina at every school holiday and during the
glorious Sicilian summers to spend time with Nonna Giovanna,
and the rest of the family. (I never met my paternal grandfather,
because he had died when Papà was fourteen.) They lovingly
viewed my brother, my mother, and me as interesting fauna with
fascinating habits to be studied. Our precise accent, our Tuscan
words, and our perfectly spoken Italian immediately shelved us
with the Others. We were from the Continent.

The Messinesi loved Mamma, especially Nonna Giovanna,
who thought that a better fate couldn't have happened to her
son, Adolfo. My mother, Luciana, was sweet and beautiful, a
placid soul and the true epitome of gentleness. Her only problem
in Messina was that often she simply couldn't understand anyone. Naturally it wasn't arduous to communicate at parties and
dinners with elegant society friends, but when it came to dealing
with the locals and the house staff, she was at a complete loss.
The Sicilian dialect is, in fact, another language, in which most
words are radically different from standard Italian. Countless
terms recall Greek, Spanish, Norman, and French, from past
invaders, with Arabic probably being the most influential of all.
Coupled with the thick local accent, this made Sicilian confusing
from every point of view.

When the cook innocently inquired, *"Cattaste u'petrosino?"* my mother panicked, knowing that she had no answer. It turned out to be only a simple request for parsley, which in Italian would have been *"Ha comprato il prezzemolo?"*

Not even a capable linguist could have avoided the ignominy my mother suffered. Once, she went to buy a *mestolo* at the local supermarket. Taking several interminable minutes to describe a ladle, she ended up surrounded by a small throng of puzzled saleswomen frantically trying to understand what the beautiful lady wanted. Finally, comprehension shone on one girl's face, who, with the pride of the true polyglot, triumphantly exclaimed: *"U'cuppino!"*

I loved spending time with Nonna Giovanna and my beautiful zia Vera, my father's younger sister. The demonstrative southern affection appealed to my gregarious tendencies. I loved being embraced by Zia Vera before she went off to one of her elegant parties, all dressed up in tulle skirts and delicate high-heeled silver sandals. Her enveloping blond hair left me dreaming about endless dancing and flirting.

But, unfortunately, Nonna Giovanna herself is not much more than a veiled but beloved memory for me. She died of cancer before I turned five. Her passing was an immense loss to all she had loved. Back home in Livorno, when my mother had to tell me of Nonna's death, she sat me on one of the big marble tables in the second-floor hall. "You know, . . . we must be happy because your nonna Giovanna is not suffering anymore and has gone to Paradise. No more medicines, no more pain. She is with God and His beautiful angels." Those words resonated inside me like unwanted notes from an alien instrument. Confronted with something much bigger than my little person, I shrank into a knot of despair. Deep emotions shook my body, mutating my heart into a foreign object, crazily pulsating incessantly. There was just one way to escape such misery: I peed in my pants.

I looked forward to the days spent visiting the other side of my father's Sicilian family, at Villa Maria in the town of Ganzirri. My grandmother's sister, Zia Stefania, had married a very wealthy man, and they had built a mansion overlooking the beautiful Straits of Messina. The gates to the property opened at the bottom of the hill, inviting the car up a winding road that seemed never to end, flanked by exotic Hawaiian plumeria trees with intensely perfumed white flowers. The hill had been transformed by the couple's enlightened vision into a botanical heaven; Zio Federico had imported tropical bushes and trees, creating a stunning landscape. Date palm trees with their wild crowns of crazy leaves nestled close to wine palms, whose trunks, encircled by formidable dangling lianas, made up the sturdy background for a profusion of colorful hibiscus shrubs. The local agave proudly displayed the prodigious growth of its one-night flowering. A voluptuous abundance of orange and red bougainvillea merged with redolent camellias and roses in an outpouring of sensual pleasure.

At the top of the hill, the road abruptly opened up into a large promenade that surrounded the house. Halfway to the villa sat a belvedere, a beautiful terrace with white marble columns that looked out over the blue Sicilian Sea, above the local villages with the magical, improbable names of Paradiso, Contemplazione, and Pace. The silvery sparkling of the waves under the bright sun dazzled those who stood at the parapet, their senses mesmerized by more than just a stunning view. A cacophony accompanied the panorama: the muffled shouts of men aboard swordfish boats motoring through the strait, the *toot, toot* of fishermen's dinghies entering the little port, the happy yelling and screaming of naked suntanned children vaulting from rock to rock, diving in and out of the warm water. Yet a great sense of peace and quiet enveloped the onlookers. The Sicilian scents, strong and powerful, penetrated the balmy air under the pine trees, jasmine bursting forth at every corner, as ubiquitous as weeds. *Zagara*—the beautiful white flower of the orange tree—pervaded the air with its subtle, but persistent smell.

The perpetual activity in the straits captivated my attention even as a small child. There was so much to observe and follow. The sturdy long fishing boats were equipped with tall masts where fishermen perched precariously on small platforms. For hours and hours they scouted the horizon, waiting for the moment to cry *"U'pisci, u'pisci,"* alerting the crew below that fish had finally been sighted. Frenzied movements would begin on the deck of the lucky boat. Like a gush of wind over a meadow, men hurried to the bow with harpoons and nets, armed for the primordial fight that has forever taken place between hunters and their mark. "This is the same fishing method employed during Homer's time," my father once whispered into my ears, bringing everything into perspective and giving free rein to my imagination.

The Greeks, the first invaders of the island, called Sicily *Thrinacria,* because of its unmistakable triangular shape. From the Ganzirri terrace at one of Sicily's three corners, one could even discern the Scylla and Charybdis that had inspired a couple of pages in the *Odyssey* and were a continual reminder that courage and perseverance eventually triumph.

Sicily is so steeped in mythology that it is impossible to exclude it from daily reality. The ferry boat line that transported people from Villa San Giovanni in Calabria to Messina was named Caronte. Who in his right mind would ever be inspired to call a passenger boat after Charon, the mournful, bad-tempered ferryman of dead souls? The ancient Charon carried the dead to Hades, crossing the somber River Styx. The Caronte Line, instead, regularly ferried thousands of happy people, merchandise, and cars back and forth over the beautiful Mediterranean Sea from the Calabria coast to the Sicilian.

My brother, sisters, and I, on our way south from Livorno, loved the moment when we boarded one of these big ferries, because it meant that our extremely long journey was finally coming to an end. In those days, we traveled by train, resignedly journeying for many long hours, incarcerated in a cramped sleeping car. As soon as our train safely transferred to the ferry, we all rushed to the upper deck to celebrate our freedom, deeply inhaling the sea air and scrutinizing the horizon for the familiar Messina skyline.

The most well-known myth in the Sicilian tradition played perfectly against the island's seasonal rhythms and its pastoral perspective. Persephone was so beautiful that her uncle Hades, Lord of the Underworld, kidnapped her and brought her down to his joyless kingdom, but her mother, Demeter, reclaimed the girl, violently protesting to Zeus. A settlement was reached: during the year Persephone would be allowed to appear on Earth for nine months, but she had to reside in the Hades for the remaining three. In Sicily, those three months represented the torrid, barren days of the summer, as opposed to winter.

Mythology infiltrated even the Sicilian sunset, when the mirage of Fata Morgana—the elusive enchantress Morgan Le Fay of King Arthur fame—seemed to distort the coast of nearby Calabria. This northern tale had been brought to the island nearly a thousand years before by the Norman conquerors and quickly adopted by the locals. On crystal clear evenings, people stopped for a few minutes to walk to the beach or a terrace to admire the sea, hoping for a sighting of Fata Morgana and the famous green ray that every so often exploded over the horizon, blurring the lines of Italy's coast.

Many people have seen it and many more have pretended; Paolo and I always rushed to the terrace, squinting out over the sea. The more I shouted, *"Oddio, che meraviglia,"* the more I was convinced I had seen the green light.

Life at Villa Maria, the beautiful Ganzirri house, was the unique result of money and good taste combined with a totally lax atmosphere. No one seemed to give a damn about anyone else, which made for a most unsettling impression. Family members acted as if they were only peripherally part of the household. Each of them seemed peculiarly uprooted, disconnected from the context of the house yet at the same time still a component.

I was utterly fascinated by the house and its inhabitants. Zia Stefania was a tall, elegant lady, the imperious president of the local Red Cross and a pillar of society. She had a voluptuous, perfumed bosom, in which she would cheerfully bury my face every time we came to visit, while covering me in great loving kisses.

Having lost her only daughter to a dramatically quick leukemia at age eleven, Zia Stefania had preserved the room of the unfortunate Maria Luisa as a kind of mausoleum, leaving everything intact. The porcelain dolls were tidily aligned in the playroom, her beautiful dresses were hung in the closet, and her favorite flowers freshly cut and arranged in the vases on her bedside table and desk. But the dark green shutters were closed and all the curtains were drawn. Every time I approached her room on the second-floor corridor, I lowered my voice. Sadness weighed heavily in those darkened quarters, where life had been switched off one spring many years before.

Zia Stefania had also created a special garden as a memorial to her beloved daughter. No one was allowed to wander there uninvited—it was surrounded by a wooden fence. Maria Luisa's garden was a heaven of tender flowers: fragile pastel irises, roses of every kind, and diaphanous sweet peas, reminders that a young, delicate life had been harvested prematurely.

Sometimes Zia Stefania took me there and I would hold her hand, squeezing tight and anxiously whispering, "Where is she now?"

"My Maria Luisa has gone to Paradise," she would answer.

I was overwhelmed by the idea that someone as young as I had been forced to leave her mother and her family, to vanish all alone. "A Paradise without my Mamma? No, thank you very much!" I thought without revealing my feelings to my grieving aunt.

Ruggero and Manfredi, her two sons, were already married and had children my age. Both were very attractive, but Ruggero looked the part of the Latin lover. Dark and tall, with strikingly handsome features and sensual lips framed by a thin mustache, he was well known for being a lady-killer.

Zia Amelia and Mademoiselle, two antediluvian ladies older than Methuselah, were also part of the Ganzirri family nucleus. Zia Amelia, a short, thin spinster aunt, had lived with the family since the 1920s. Mademoiselle, the children's former nanny, had become so much a part of the family that she never went back to France, remaining at Villa Maria until death claimed her at the whopping age of ninety-something. Both ladies were the proud repositories of the house keys, which they wore on chains around their waists. The keys clanked and jangled, advertising their owners' whereabouts throughout the house.

"*Mademoiselle! Où sont les clés?*" yelled Zia Stefania at the completely deaf old lady.

"*Quoi?*" she shrieked back.

"*Le chiavi!* She wants the keys!" interjected Zia Amelia, barking her instructions, squinting to see better which key to select.

I never discovered what this arsenal opened and closed, but both ladies certainly seemed very busy at all times. I was a little afraid of Zia Amelia and kept my distance from her long whooshing skirts. Always dressed in black, she inspected the world with some haughtiness, conveying disapproval of all that surrounded her. Later, I realized that her vinegary expression was due to her near-blindness.

A beautiful porch ran around the perimeter of the house, allowing for lazy al fresco lunches and dinners during even the hottest summer months. Wicker chairs draped with colorful pillows and shawls were scattered around, and it was here that the ladies sat, sipping tea and working on their crocheting, knitting, or embroidery. Children played under the relaxed supervision of the adults.

My favorite activity was peeling *fichi d'India,* the weird prickly pears that grow in every corner of Sicily. Zia Gabriella, Ruggero's beautiful wife, used to organize "peeling races," turning those much-resented good table manners into competitive tools. I always volunteered, eager to prove my prowess. The process required a fork, a knife, and some dexterity, accompanied by a good dose of boldness. With a fork in my left hand, I pierced the juicy fruit. Holding it down firmly, I first cut away the two ends and then drew two deep horizontal incisions. Having done that, the task was practically accomplished, and I swiftly detached the skin from the flesh with just a little help from my knife. I had achieved my primary goal: none of the infinitesimal yet terribly painful thorns had pricked my hands.

The winner earned the pride of being responsible for the pyramid of perfectly stunning oval fruits piled high on a tray and served at the end of dinner in all their polychromatic glory. My tongue loved the challenge of savoring each little seed of the *fico d'India,* lost in the watery, almost watermelon-like pulp; for me the pleasure of eating it resided mainly in its granular texture. I relished the bizarre sensation of gulping down hundreds of those firm seeds kept together by coarse flesh. But first I had to get through dinner.

At the table in the large formal dining room, no one listened to anyone else. Disagreement was standard, conversations were aimed at no one in particular, and it was common practice to interrupt a discussion with an abrupt change of subject. At times, the beautiful wood-paneled room would become eerily silent, the person who had spoken last turned into the unwilling center of attention.

"Ah! I remember when my grandfather owned the largest sulphur mines in Sicily. Those were the days . . . even the Palermo *Mafiosi* respected our family. Did I ever tell you . . ." Zia Stefania proffered.

"*Minchia!* Mamma, who cares?" Ruggero answered, using the most vulgar Sicilian expletive. All eyes turned immediately toward my mother, who sat uneasily in her chair. She straightened herself and checked to see if Paolo and I had heard. My Continental Family was not accustomed to such verbal eruptions, and it was with some wicked pleasure that everyone else at the table, including Zio and Zia, viewed the results on our deepening crimson cheeks. Giggles burst forth, but sotto voce.

Often Zia Stefania launched into long-winded descriptions of operas she had just attended. Having once entertained hopes of becoming a singer herself, she talked about the most recondite meanings of *La Traviata* and *Tosca*. *"Ah, l'aria di Alfredo . . ."*

"Luciana, would you like to know my secret recipe for the best *granita di caffè?"* Zia Amelia would interject, having heard nothing of the previous exchange.

"Minchia! Idda sodda è! She is deaf!" Ruggero exclaimed, once again reverting to Sicilian. Biagio, the faithful butler, continued to shuffle around the table unperturbed.

While conversation at the Villa Maria table was often disconcerting, food remained an active bond between all the various family members. There was never controversy over the splendid dishes. The *pasta al pomodoro* was typically Italian, yet so different in taste from Emilia's. Tomatoes in Sicily were redder than anywhere else; they guzzle the intense sun, transforming that energy into a darker, plumper flesh. The cooks generously season their sauce with the intensely pungent Sicilian olive oil, topping it all off—my favorite touch—with several slices of eggplant, slivered and fried to perfection. I so enjoyed biting into those succulent wedges, their borders browned and barely firm enough to hold in place the juicy flesh.

As in everything else, Sicilians had their own version of pasta history. It was said to have been invented by the Greek invaders, who called it *makaria* and offered it at funerals. The sun, the balmy air, and the fabulous produce that grew on this blessed island must have ignited creativity.

In Ganzirri, spaghetti, penne, ziti, farfalle, and lasagne all came to life after they were married to some unique ingredients: *pasta cu la muddica* was made with bread crumbs and anchovies; ziti with broccoli; penne with pancetta and *caciocavallo* cheese; spaghetti with squid and its marvelous ink sauce; farfalle with zucchini and bell peppers; *timballo di maccheroni* (baked maca-roni pie) with eggplant and ricotta. Olives, pine nuts, capers, eggplant, saffron, and fennel were the omnipresent elements of Sicilian culinary chemistry, heightening the flavors.

Swordfish was often the main component of meals. There are infinite and imaginative ways of preparing it, as it has always been a staple of Sicilian cuisine. My favorites were *involtini*, mouthwatering little rolls made of tender slices of fish filled with an amalgam of spicy provolone cheese, onions, basil, bread crumbs and the fish trimmings, all having been sautéed in olive oil. I also loved swordfish topped with *salmoriglio—u'sammorig-ghiu* in Sicilian dialect—the ubiquitous tangy green sauce that accompanied all kinds of meat, fish, and vegetables. It contained the essence of the Island of the Sun—extra-virgin olive oil, water, fresh oregano, lemon, and parsley.

✤ *Salmoriglio* ✤
HERBED LEMON AND
OLIVE OIL SAUCE

This is excellent with grilled tuna or swordfish or Steamed Cod (page 151). And, thank God, this sauce recipe doesn't go crazy! *Non impazzisce!*

1 ½ cups extra-virgin olive oil
½ cup hot water
Juice of 2 lemons
1 tablespoon chopped flat-leaf parsley
1 teaspoon oregano
Salt and freshly ground pepper *a piacere*

Pour the olive oil into a bowl. Whisk in the hot water and lemon juice, and add the parsley, oregano, and salt and pepper. Serve warm.

Makes about 2 cups

Spitini would have been another of my choices had I been invited to order my meal. They were nothing more that simple skewers of rolled veal, but the way they were prepared is forever engraved in my culinary memory. They had a kind of smoky taste, probably due to the combination of *caciocavallo,* the powerful Sicilian cheese, and the many fresh herbs and bread crumbs that composed the filling. Their arrival at the dinner table always filled me with delicious anticipation.

And naturally, *la caponata,* the queen of all vegetable dishes! It called for celery and eggplant, cut into small cubes, quickly fried separately, and thrown into a seriously intense tomato sauce. The sauce itself had to simmer over a low flame for several hours, to combine the flavor of tomatoes with black olives and capers, a pinch of local fresh oregano contributing to its spicy, summery flavor. Red pepper, pungent basil leaves, and a little bit of sugar and vinegar were often added, sometimes with a couple of canned anchovies. Sicily's thousands of "authentic" recipes prove that *caponata* has as many personifications as there are cooks. It was a sociological lesson and a culinary adventure to eat at friends' houses, as they would usually announce that Nicolino, Maria, or Giuseppe—whoever reigned over the kitchen—was serving the absolute paradigm of *la caponata Siciliana!*

Caponatina alla Mia Maniera

My Eggplant and Celery Caponata

This is a relatively quick recipe, which I call *caponatina* (the suffix *ina* meaning "small") because it cuts many corners but still produces exquisite results. It is a good dish to prepare a day—or even a couple of days—ahead. Keep it in the refrigerator and bring it to room temperature before serving. It is perfect by itself or as an accompaniment to meat.

3 pounds eggplants (about 3 to 4), peeled
1 bunch celery
1 cup sunflower oil
Salt and freshly ground pepper *a piacere*
3 medium yellow onions
3 tablespoons extra-virgin olive oil
1 cup red wine vinegar or balsamic vinegar
2 tablespoons sugar
2 cups Emilia's Tomato Sauce (page 5)
1 cup black olives, pitted and halved
2 tablespoons capers
½ teaspoon dried oregano

Cut the eggplants and celery into ½-inch cubes. Heat the sunflower oil in a deep frying pan over medium-high heat. When the oil is hot—about 350°F—fry the celery and then the eggplant in batches, taking care not to crowd the pan, until golden, about 5 minutes per batch. Drain well, season with salt and pepper, and set aside.

Peel and finely chop the onion. Sauté in the olive oil in a

large saucepan over medium heat, stirring until soft and translucent, about 8 to 10 minutes. Add the vinegar and sugar, lower the heat, and simmer for about 10 minutes, or until about half of the liquid has evaporated.

Stir in the tomato sauce, olives, capers, oregano, and the eggplant and celery cubes. Remove from the heat and let cool to room temperature.

Makes 10 servings

The great *Feste del Santo Padrone* (Feast of the Patron Saints) and all annual festivities, sacred or secular, were excuses for complete immersion in Sicilian sounds and colors, perfumes, and sumptuous costumes. How different from Livorno! Any of the innumerable processions through small and big towns exemplified the blazing, intense emotions that characterized the Sicilian population, providing a quick snapshot of its ancient traditions and culture. My favorite was *La Festa dei Due Giganti*, the August celebration of the two giants, who were said to have founded the city of Messina. The immense plaster statues—Mata, the white woman, and her husband, Grifone, the dark-skinned Moor—were paraded through the streets in their gaudy colorful costumes to be admired by all, then finally parked in the center of town near City Hall. I looked up at them with awe, defying the fierce look in the Moor's face and the equally untamed expression in his wife's. "*Guarda, Paolo!* Look at their bodies! Do you think they could catch us easily with those humongous legs and hands?" I whispered, squeezing his hand.

Each August 15, hundreds of penitents—men and women in

various states of undress to underscore their sacrificial enthusiasm—followed *La Vara,* a wooden float surmounted by a huge
construction of angels, clouds, and gold. From atop this fantastic
expression of religious architecture rose a papier-mâché Christ,
ready to launch His Mother, Maria, to the ultimate happiness of
heaven. Since *varare* means "to launch a boat," the name couldn't
have been more appropriate for the Day of the Assumption. The
festivities continued for three full days, with the entire population out spilling into squares and streets, until it ended with the
deafening eruption of fireworks over the straits.

I loved *i fruttini di marzapane,* one of the best Sicilian inventions, sweet and nutty, a pleasure to bite into, a joy to behold,
and the gourmet link to every Sicilian holiday. Marzipan's mal-
leable dough, made of almonds and sugar paste, was worked into
all kinds of fruit and vegetable shapes: precisely formed tomatoes
as red as those in the market; tiny eggplants, their dark purple-
ness seeming to have captured the intensity of the sun; oddly
shaped bell peppers every centimeter as real as the ones found in
the kitchen pantry; and prickly pears, peaches, celery, walnuts,
oranges, figs, and pomegranates. Apples and oranges perched
next to delicate grapes and tiny bananas, to whose skin the clever
pasticciere had even added realistic imperfections. Some of the
fruits looked as if they'd just recently been bitten into by a
greedy epicurean.

Fruttini di marzapane filled the little *carretto siciliano,* the perfect emblem of Sicilian culture, art, and everyday life. The cart's
flanks were painted with the ancient tales of Moors and Paladins,
and fabled battles of the crusaders against the unfaithful Sara-
cens. The horse in front wore a splendid headdress of multicolored feathers and red trim, bordered with little gold mirrors, that
decorated its body from proud head to tail. As a child, I could

have spent hours looking through Billè's windows, the famous *pasticceria* in Messina, salivating and marveling at the *fruttini's* perfection.

While Billé was the place for extravagant holiday confections, Irrera a Mare was the great bar-*pasticceria* overlooking the straits where every Messinese went on Sunday after Mass. From its garden terrace, one could comfortably inspect the entire Sicilian and Calabrian coasts, with their continuous traffic of ferry boats. Going to Irrera satisfied every generation's needs: the adults could relax and enjoy their sweet breakfast treats, comfortably seated at old iron tables under the trees, and children could play in the dust and dirt without much supervision.

At Irrera a Mare, I first discovered the meaning of "paradise of the senses." Even at an early age, I was aware that new gates of bliss had opened up for me. I felt the exhilaration of dipping my brioche, as light as a delicate cirrus cloud, velvety and not too sweet, into my *granita*. In the relaxed tempo of Sicilian life, I loved to stare at the blue sea, framed by the forbidding agave and the sumptuous bougainvillea. My heart slowly filled with a deep sense of thankfulness for being alive and able to savor such extraordinary delight.

❧ Granita di Caffè ❧
COFFEE GRANITA

Granita di caffè con panna, often with *panna montata,* is the perfect Sicilian breakfast. A classic brioche—amber colored, slightly orange flavored, and still warm from the oven—is dipped into cold grainy *granita* and served with a small cloud of whipped cream on top. This is Mamma's recipe, *a prova di bomba!* as we say in Italian. Foolproof! Great for summer days—morning or afternoon—it can be made ahead of time.

Fruits, such as strawberries, lemons, or peaches, can be substituted for the coffee and all make exquisite *granite*. Just peel and seed the fruit, cut it into chunks, and puree it in a food processor. Add enough water to make the puree liquid.

4 cups strong black coffee
1 cup water
Sugar *a piacere*
2 cups (1 pint) heavy cream
6 slices brioche

Mix together the coffee and water, add sugar to taste, and stir until dissolved. Pour the liquid into a nonreactive baking pan, preferably lightweight stainless steel. Put it in the freezer. After 30 minutes, or once the mixture has started to crystallize, stir vigorously with a metal spoon. Repeat the stirring 3 or 4 more times, every 30 minutes. When the mixture has frozen completely, scrape it with a metal spoon until the crystals combine into an icy, sorbetlike mixture.

Whip the cream until it holds soft peaks.

Serve the granita in individual cups or crystal glasses, topped with the whipped cream and with a slice of brioche on the side.

Makes 6 servings

Livorno Today

The covered market in Livorno

A few years ago, I found myself back in Livorno on a hot summer day for the wedding of my youngest cousin, Alessandra. It was to be a simple ceremony, but all the uncles, cousins, and aunts had decided to show up en masse to celebrate her happiness. For me, it was also a great excuse to spend some time with my mother and to enjoy, after many years, a large family gathering at my aunt's home.

In just one sweep, my gaze took in a panorama of the familiar details from my childhood. I saw Nonna Valentina's inlaid vitrine, the elegant cabinet that had lodged her beautiful collection of antique glasses. Silver-framed pictures recorded the past with loving care. The images of weddings, First Communions, christenings, picnics, sailing trips, and mountain excursions overwhelmed me with emotion. I had come home.

"I am staying longer," I informed my mother. I decided to gather my memories and size them up with reality. I wanted to hurry out to stroll in the sunny streets and squares. I wanted to eat another *frate*—the famous doughnut of my school days—in Piazza Cavallotti, near the market, and I craved the food Emilia had introduced me to forty-five years before.

I had returned to Livorno many times throughout my adult life, but had always been constrained by my primary goal of sitting down with my grandmother. I would arrive and sprawl on the sofa under the living room window, asking questions, probing for details, and storing precious information in my heart. Maroon leather albums, full of black-and-white pictures and sepia portraits, were neatly stacked next to her armchair. The photographs faithfully illustrated Nonna Valentina's oft-recounted stories. In one, Nonno GianPaolo smiles from the veranda of the Mombassa Tennis Club, wearing his white flannel trousers, and reclining nonchalantly on a wicker chaise longue. In another, Luciana leans against her two strong brothers, Marcello and Pierluigi, piercing the air with the gaze from her periwinkle eyes, bravely fighting her shyness in front of the camera. About seven or eight, she wears the beautiful lace collar that later graced my elegant dresses and those of my sisters.

At the time of Alessandra's wedding, Nonna had been dead for two years, having passed away just after turning one hundred. Now I was in Livorno without her.

The day after I arrived, Mamma and I got into my battered Ford station wagon and drove into Livorno from Ardenza, the quaint seaside area where my mother now lives. We followed the beautiful road that stretches all the way from Antignano, the southern point of Livorno, to the ancient part of the city. What a magnificent coast: The great expanse of the Tyrrhenian Sea, with its insolent blue, was dotted here and there by majestic ships and solemn oil tankers crisscrossing the water between Livorno and the world. Hundreds of smaller vessels joined in this crowd of sea cruisers. Graceful sailing boats with frenzied multicolored spinnakers and billowing white sails drew geometric designs through the waves, tacking and racing against each other. Fishing boats sped quickly out of sight, pressed to reach their hunting positions. Slow tugboats trudged up and down, blowing their horns to signal their presence.

The promenade, lined by fragrant pittosporum bushes and blooming fuchsia oleander, was crowded with families. Everyone walked slowly in the sultry afternoon, carrying beach umbrellas and chairs and licking the ubiquitous ice cream cones.

The Livornesi have always loved their warm season. As soon as spring delivers the first sunny days, everyone starts working on their swimming muscles and well-oiled tans. Livorno turns into a gigantic beach for swimmers and sun worshipers. The beautiful local ladies immediately shed as many clothes as they can, and modesty disappears from their lexicon, miniskirts and tight shorts, flimsy wraps and invisible bikinis becoming the daily mode of dress. No one seems to mind. The men think nothing of walking around shirtless; what is the point in exercising extensively if you can't show off your deltoids? Very often heavy gold chains bedeck their hairy masculine chests. Skins darken as fast as new daisies grow in the fields.

On that summer day, my mother and I observed, with affectionate incredulity, our fellow citizens. Cigarettes casually dangled, in every stage of consumption, from lips parted over splendidly white teeth. *"Ma come faranno mai?"* I asked my mother in disbelief. How did they do it? How did they manage to look so healthy and athletic while chain-smoking? We had no answers, so we decided to walk for a few minutes along the promenade. The young people fascinated me most.

"The coarseness and uncouthness of the new generation is appalling," I muttered, a sympathetic echo resounding from my mother. "Look at those two!" I pointed at two attractive girls who were resting their tired limbs on the low wall that runs along the promenade, parallel to the seacoast. They displayed with pride two great pairs of unbridled breasts, covered so scantily as to leave very little to the imagination. One wore short black socks and combat boots; the other teetered atop improbably high platform shoes. Their dog, a big brown mutt, roamed defiantly, without a leash. Some of the boys in the big group surrounding them sported very long hair, of every unlikely color and shade, while others displayed impressively shaved craniums. A huge number of motorbikes, Vespas and Hondas, huddled together in the middle of the street or slumbered nonchalantly against the wall, ready to be ridden by these modern centaurs. The girls each straddled a roaring bike, their miniskirts and shorts revealing perfectly shaped buttocks that by now had reached—thanks to the unforgiving sun—the color of ripe eggplants. With a great roaring of engines, off they went in the carefree happiness of youth.

Horrified by my judgmental attitude, I looked at my mother. It was an unnerving moment of déjà vu. I realized that I had sounded exactly like my grandfather. His voice echoed in my ears: *"Ma ti immagini, Valentina?"* he would say to my grandmother. "I saw a girl today wearing trousers! How can her mother be so permissive?" I remember being furious at his quick judgments based solely on appearances. And here I was, years later, just as shamelessly condemning the younger generation.

Mamma and I gazed at the sea, taking in the loveliness of a cloudless summer day, the familiar silhouettes of faraway islands emerging from the waters. Livorno's coastline enthralled us with its wild beauty; instead of sandy beaches or gentle approaches to the water, an imposing barrier of untamed rocks, dark and crested, showcased the perfect transparency of a cobalt sea. My mother informed me that after World War II the overzealous American authorities had mistakenly declared our seacoast off-limits, a polluted hazard to their soldiers' health. "Their loss!" She shook her head, gazing at the wild stretch of rocks that lay before our eyes, punctuated here and there by little dark ponds of clear water.

My feet were always bruised when, as a child, I jumped from rock to rock fishing for transparent shrimp or collecting *patelle,* the little clams that stuck to the rocks in crevices and refused to be moved. I favored the little ruddy *gangilli,* in the Livorno dialect, with their twisted slim shells. These sea mollusks bravely pushed out their antennae from their secure univalve housing, and vehemently wiggled their spindly red legs in protest of my efforts to relocate them.

On that sunny June afternoon, it seemed as if nothing had

changed from the summer days of my childhood. Children still squatted silently, inspecting the little ponds that the currents had created in the chasms between the rocks. I knew so well what they were doing! They were hoping to catch one of those fickle crabs that—with implausible speed—always manage to escape, sliding sideways toward safety. The beautiful sea anemones and the red starfish are the most difficult catch, and triumphant shrieks summoned mothers and families when an enterprising child captured one.

Mamma and I drove past the naval academy, a beautiful late-nineteenth-century complex of buildings where future young officers of the Italian navy are trained. This is a significant point of reference in my family's life. Here my father had studied and subsequently taught, and here my heart had ticked its first romantic beats.

"*Un gelato?*" I asked my mother, hoping to entice her into an impromptu stop at the Baracchina, the simple quasi shack that annoyingly destroys the symmetry and elegance of Piazza Sant' Jacopo in Acquaviva. The *gelato* there is very good, but I had a personal agenda, a special remembrance to observe and some past embarrassments to exorcise. This was the place where I would take up position to ambush the poor unsuspecting cadets on their off-duty days. I consumed endless *gelati,* just hoping to glimpse the current object of my attentions. I'd hide behind the enormous ice cream cones, nonchalantly walking back and forth between the immense iron gates and the bus stop, the path selected by my would-be prey as they proceeded toward their free afternoons. Sometimes I managed to bump casually into my target, at which point I'd feel really lucky if even a sparkle of blasé recognition registered in his eyes. Alas, a conspicuous invisibility followed me everywhere, like the *ombra* on the marble terrace. My mother and I briefly walked the square, laughing at the memories of my tortured afternoons and enjoying our *amaretto* and coffee *gelato* cones: "*Ricordi Fabio? E Ascanio?* They looked so handsome in their blue uniforms."

Mamma pointed at the beautiful sixteenth-century church, oriented toward the sea, with its apse reaching out as if preaching to the sailors themselves. One of the lasting visual memories of my Livorno school days is the little gray church of Sant' Jacopo in winter, splashed by the gigantic waves that pound the coast, driven by the merciless *Libeccio.* The tempestuous soaring of the Mediterranean Sea is linked to my first introduction to the great Livornese sport of grandiose swearing. As the history books won't tell you, this is a highly respected and constantly refined skill in my hometown. The square, where Mamma and I now stood, was on the bus route to my high school. During the bad season, we often saw the salty marine spray drape the bus windshield in white foam, obliterating the driver's view. In those precise moments, if lucky enough to be sitting within earshot, we young passengers were given an expletive crash course. (At that time, within Italy, a battle continued between the heathen Communists and the sainted Christian Democrats. Since the free-spirited Livornesi prided themselves on being inordinately passionate Communists, they indulged in the worst possible blasphemous outbursts to trumpet their independence from the Church. After all, it was in our city that the Italian Communist Party was founded in 1921.)

The title of *porco* (pig) was often attributed to the Virgin Mary and any other saint who seemed to tickle the driver's fancy. Even worse designations were casually slapped on every kind of holy matter: the Holy Roman Catholic Church and its dogmas, beliefs, angels, archangels, and Holy Spirit were all fair targets. All kinds of names from the zoological universe were cleverly doled out and matched to God, Jesus Christ, and the poor Madonna, who seemed to attract the most affectionate, nonsensical insults. *"Madonna tremota in sur 'ciuo zoppo!* Earthquake-devastated Madonna on a lame donkey!" the bus driver would exclaim, braking abruptly to avoid an oncoming car.

The following morning, I was anxious to visit the *mercato coperto,* the daily covered market where Emilia and I had spent so much time. One of Livorno's architectural glories, this beautiful and imposing structure was erected in 1894, a marvel of modern building technique. Hosting two hundred stands and thirty-four stores, it also had subterranean refrigerator cells and a variety of office facilities, a very modern concept for the time. I crossed the bridge over the antique canal and stood in front of the ocher facade adorned with elaborate Corinthian columns. Volutes, rosettes, and acanthus leaves framed the huge wide-open portals, as a considerable crowd flowed in and out. Walking in, I was immediately surprised by how vivid and accurate my memory of the place was. "Look at the skylight!" I gasped, staring once again at the extraordinary thirty-five-meter-high structure of glass and elaborate wrought-iron work. Daylight streamed in, illuminating the chaotic scene beneath, even in bad weather. The fervor, the cacophony, the pushing and shoving were still the same. All self-respecting vendors shouted at the top of their lungs, touting the marvelous qualities of their products.

I walked everywhere, admiring the beautiful merchandise. Tender fennel, with its fluffy tops; dark green zucchini, the pride and pleasure of the Livornesi table, as small as fingers; diminutive string beans; and all sorts of other greens were piled in heaps and stacks. Clusters of red tomatoes still on the vine, picked only hours before, exuded their particular pungent scent, musky, with an intensely spicy twist. Earthenware containers holding all kinds of pickled olives, onions, and capers sat near colorful baskets of spices.

Cascades of sausages and salamis hung from wires suspended above the stalls. Cheeses of different types and brands were stacked and displayed in masterly pyramids; smelly *pecorini* of every conceivable variety advertised themselves as products of small villages a few kilometers away or from farther regions. White *mozzarelle,* barely arrived from Naples, swam in their milk, skewered by a blunt sign that screamed *"Fresche!"* at the shoppers. I watched the saleswomen behind the counter—beautiful young girls dressed in pristine white uniforms—as they cut and sliced huge or small wheels of delicious cheeses, careful as surgeons in an operating room. Suggestions were given and highly specialized information exchanged about the pros and cons of this or that product. "This Parmesan cheese is from 1996, choose it!" recommended a girl in a starched lace cap, whose serene face recalled a Raffaello Madonna. It was like talking to a high priestess. Cheese, like wine, has its own superior cuvées, and we buyers should pay attention.

I started tasting and discussing the virtues of the microscopic green beans. I too clamored for attention, bargaining over every fruit or vegetable, pooh-poohing prices, and throwing in counteroffers before finally feigning walking away with a resigned shrug of my shoulders. In other words, I played Emilia and proudly saved a couple of precious *lire!* My mother tried to slow me down, since our daily plans included several incursions into the local restaurant scene and not a lot of cooking. *"Calma, calma,"* she pleaded.

Outside the covered market, where other kinds of merchandise were sold, I had another agenda. I couldn't live without a pair of *zoccoletti,* the wooden slides that had been forbidden to me as a child by Mamma and Nonna, my fashion police. Like a hound, I bounded to the stands that offered mountains of them in every possible color and fabric and leather, piled haphazardly atop wooden planks. I chose and bargained and paid, finally emerging with my very own *volgare* possession, happy to be finally in step with the rest of my fellow citizens.

"*Il lupo perde il pelo ma non il vizio.* But this leopard would not change her spots," Mamma commented dryly, rolling her eyes. I moved to an exciting heap of dresses, skirts, sweaters, trousers, and jackets that were advertised on sale for a few liras each. The owner of this particular stand shouted with a thunderous voice: "*Rufolate, oh donne, rufolate!*" repeating, mantra-like, "Go on rooting, women, go on!" I froze. He described exactly what I was doing! Equating me to a rooting pig cast a blow to my self-esteem. I looked around to see if anyone in the surrounding female crowd had actually heard those words, but no one had moved an eyebrow, hands still dug through rags, attention solely focused on the possibility of a great find.

My pilgrimage wouldn't have been complete without a visit to the place where Adriano, the old *frati* maker, had once turned out his delicacies. I already knew that he had been gone for quite some time, but I wasn't prepared to discover—nor imagined it possible—that someone else now sold *frati* that competed in perfection. The store, though still a hole in the wall, was now splendidly modern, and hygiene reigned supreme. The coating of sprinkled sugar stuck to my upper lip, the doughnut melted in my mouth, and its delicious taste filled the tiny solitary space that for so many decades had been awaiting this moment: a triumphant reunion of memory and taste buds.

Mamma and I dedicated the afternoon to visiting Il Convento del Sacro Cuore and our old house. My old school had changed a great deal. The real estate frenzy of the last thirty years had devoured the garden, engulfing trees and bushes. Modernization had transformed the school into a strident assortment of metal and glass, the plain old buildings incongruously incorporated into a confusion of contemporary constructions. Electric garage gates intercepted our walk to the old reception area, and glass-paneled doors enclosed an entrance to a new tall condominium. I briefly glimpsed the chapel from behind a forbidding new wall. A gentle-looking nun met us, inquiring, "Would you like to come in?"

"*Sia lodato Gesù Cristo.* May Jesus Christ be praised," I whispered in reply, suddenly surprised by the proper salutation resurrected from my Catholic school days. "I studied here," I said spontaneously. "I would be so happy to see the convent again."

"*Ma sicuro!*" she responded, quickly directing us to Sister Fernanda's office.

My mother's eyes opened wide: *Suor Fernanda?* "She must be a hundred years old! She was *my* teacher!" Mamma blurted.

Not a single wrinkle on her nonagenarian face, Sister Fernanda looked up expectantly from behind her busy desk, her eyes shining with intelligence and curiosity behind a pair of wire-rimmed glasses, her skin glowing a delicate pink. Sister Fernanda was the school's official scribe, recording facts and events with her precise, beautiful handwriting, keeping everything for posterity.

As she led us around on an impromptu tour of the old and new buildings, Sister Fernanda seemed very proud of the architectural massacre perpetrated upon my school. The narrow corridors appeared to be the only remnant from my time, as dark and somber as ever. I bent to examine the coat hangers hung at the usual lilliputian height, discovering that they had not changed: the wooden pegs were still surmounted by the peculiar happy tin face of Aeolus. I checked the God of Winds's plump cheeks, making sure that they had kept blowing, his rotund mouth forming a surprised *"Oh!"* eternally puffing into imponderable space. "You are still here!" I murmured.

"An earthquake weakened the church," Sister Fernanda informed us, opening the heavy doors that led inside. She genuflected, her white robe sweeping the tiles, her dark wooden rosary clinking against the floor. "We were forced to rebuild it." I looked around in dismay at the ghastly modernity that incorporated salvaged parts of the old building, including pieces of the old altar now decorating the new walls. Contemporary stained-glass windows replaced the beautiful polychromatic ones I remembered. An elongated, arched red blot that suspiciously resembled a hot red pepper turned out to signify the blood of Jesus Christ. I decided to keep silent, hiding my true sentiments behind charitable *"Mms!"* of neutral appreciation.

Thankfully, the little altar of the Madonna was the same one of my childhood, her blue mantle beautifully restored, her sweet eyes gazing at me with celestial kindness. I knelt before her and remembered the *fioretti* that for so many days of so many Mays had occupied the creative side of my brain. "What could I give up today in order to gain plenary indulgence?" I asked myself. What kindness would receive Sister Agnese's seal of approval?

As if she had read my mind, Sister Fernanda produced Sister Agnese's death picture, *il santino* as we say in Italian, and offered it to me. I concentrated on her lovely, serene features. Her usual smile illuminated her face; her eyes twinkled with humor behind her glasses.

"Neanche una ruga! Once again, not a visible wrinkle!" I cried out.

What was the secret of these saintly women? They seemed cloned, their faces untouched, engaging their interlocutors with wit and intelligence. Did prayers yield an everlasting beautiful complexion? Did the convent nuns follow a special spiritual diet? Did serenity result from their religious beliefs? There was surely one exception, I thought to myself: I bet Sister Jacopina died with a crumpled face, trillions of lines crisscrossing it in a tangle of nastiness!

At the end of our visit, Sister Fernanda drew my mother and me into a warm embrace. Her voice breaking, she said, *"Tornate, tornate per piacere.* Come back to visit, please."

Toward the end of the afternoon, Mamma and I came upon our old house, situated in the center of the city. Externally, it still looked pretty much the same, but I knew that it had been divided into several apartments after my grandparents had sold it. The pristine warm peach facade provided a perfect backdrop to the architectural details that had been cleverly repainted a contrasting cream. The big old door was still there, as imposing as ever, two massive walnut panels with their prominent brass knobs centered in carved acanthus leaves. Alas! Emilia no longer presided over its care, and the knobs, her great pride and joy, had completely lost their luster. So many fingerprints dulled their surface; Emilia would have been horrified to witness this neglect. Nevertheless, I realized that the house, a restrained example of nineteenth-century neoclassical style, was still beautiful. Thankfully the original architect had avoided indulging in too many distracting accents, as the fashion of those times dictated. Two pilasters ran perpendicularly through the building and their elaborate Corinthian capitals ended under an arched pediment. This particular architectural detail had always been one of my favorite elements, as it reminded me of the wooden construction blocks with which I used to play. Half-shell ornaments still adorned the tall second-floor windows. I'd always considered them integral parts of some extravagant fantasy. A mermaid, at minimum, should have emerged from those shells. "*Prima o poi, uno di questi giorni.* Sooner or later, one of these days," I would say to soothe myself every night in those blissful moments before falling asleep.

I had hoped to see my beloved magnolia tree again, but we learned that when the house was sold the new owners—real estate developers—quickly replaced it, and the garage, with a gray cement apartment building. The entire garden had been destroyed, and large blank walls delineated the new tenants' parking spaces. No more rosemary bushes or bitter orange trees, no more flower beds, no more chickens or cats, no more games of marbles. Mamma and I stood silent. There was not much to say.

❧ *Cacciucco* ❧
LIVORNO FISH SOUP

The faces one encounters in the streets, in the markets, and on the piers of Livorno are nothing short of Felliniesque. These are the faces of people who live at full speed. Plentiful pronounced wrinkles and deep suntans have carved their features with determination. Livorno's population is the heritage of not only ancient pirates, but also the myriad brigands and inmates that Cosimo I, a Medici duke, freed from Florence jails to build an important new port city on the Mediterranean. Some say that *cacciucco,* the strongly flavored fish soup that is famous in my hometown, is a perfect analogy for the Livornesi themselves. A great, hearty mixture of creatures from near and far seas, cooked together in a large cauldron, and served with the knowledge that pleasure derives from diversity.

Emilia used to say, "A *cacciucco* is not a real *cacciucco* unless it contains a *scorfano!*" the ugly red scorpion fish, a monster—as the name proclaims—that hides under the rocks in the Tyhrrenian Sea. It is a big russet creature, with a tremendous protruding chin, bulging eyes, and a hideous grimace. Cleaning it is labor-intensive: its body is covered with menacing spikes that can easily hurt inexpert hands. "*Bimba,* remember first to plunge the fish in ice water, you will clean its scales much faster," Emilia recommended. Nowadays I simplify and buy filleted fish. Keep in mind that you needn't gather every fish on the list; what's important is to have a good variety.

½ pound clams
½ pound mussels
2 pounds skinless fish fillets, such as scorpion fish—
    if you can find it—mullet, and monkfish
1 pound octopus
1 pound cleaned squid or cuttlefish
½ pound large shelled shrimp
1 medium yellow onion
1 large carrot
3 cloves garlic
½ stalk celery

⅔ cup plus 1 teaspoon extra-virgin olive oil

1 bay leaf

1 sprig rosemary

Pinch of red pepper flakes

Salt and freshly ground pepper *a piacere*

1 cup dry white wine

4 ripe tomatoes or one 14-ounce can crushed tomatoes

1 tablespoon chopped flat-leaf parsley

12 thick slices bread, toasted and rubbed with garlic,
	for serving

Put the clams and mussels in a large basin of cold water. Change the water several times, until it is no longer sandy. Scrape the shells clean with a brush or the back of a knife. Rinse again. Pull off the stringy beards attached to the mussels. Rinse again and set aside.

Rinse and pat dry the fish, octopus, squid, and shrimp. Cut the octopus and squid into 2-inch chunks.

Peel and finely chop the onion, carrot, and garlic. Finely chop the celery. Sauté the vegetables in ⅔ cup of the olive oil in a large stockpot over medium heat. Add the bay leaf, rosemary, red pepper flakes, and salt and pepper. Cook, stirring, until the vegetables begin to soften, about 5 minutes. Remove and discard the bay leaf.

Add the octopus and squid to the pot, along with the wine and tomatoes. Cook over low heat for about 15 minutes, until the octopus and squid are al dente. Use a slotted spoon to remove the octopus and squid from the pot, and set them aside on a plate.

Add the fish to the pot and cook for about 15 minutes, until just cooked through.

While the fish is cooking, throw the clams and mussels into a large frying pan with the remaining 1 teaspoon olive oil, and set over high heat. Cover and cook, shaking the pan, until the shells open, 3 to 5 minutes. Throw away any shellfish that remains closed. Remove the clams and mussels from their shells and discard the shells.

Return the octopus and squid to the pot and add the shrimp, clams, and mussels. Cook for another 10 minutes, then stir in the parsley.

Put the garlic-rubbed toasts into individual terra-cotta bowls, and ladle a generous portion of *cacciucco* on top of each.

Makes 12 servings

My grandfather didn't approve of *cacciucco*. Its fiery taste and unrefined looks were the antithesis of my family's culinary credo. Furthermore, it contains garlic and onions, ingredients Nonno disliked and had formally banned from his table. I shudder to think of the task that had weighed upon Emilia's capable shoulders. How could she have made an interesting meal without the essential help of those humble ingredients? How could a good cook produce meals that bordered on complete blandness?

"Emilia, non c'è'aglio qui dentro vero?" Nonno would sniff suspiciously at the arrival of some particularly appealing dish. If the pasta looked a little bit too rustic, if its appeal seemed too daring, the redness of the sauce too loud, his immense white eyebrows arched. "No traces of garlic or onion here, eh?"

I still smile when I think of how my grandfather loved to visit me, many years later, when I lived in Rome. We followed a routine: the first evening we ate dinner in a fancy restaurant. *"Semel in anno licet insanire!* Once in a while it is nice to do something outrageous!"* Nonno would announce, holding open the door of the expensive and famous place where he proudly entertained his eldest granddaughter. We enjoyed our wonderful tête-à-tête, meeting precisely at seven to eat our dinner at seven-thirty. Nonno's goodnight kiss was inexorably stamped on my cheeks one hour later, on the dot.

The following night, I would invite him to my apartment. The first time he accepted my dinner invitation, I took care to prepare unpalatable (to me) recipes, dutifully avoiding the forbidden ingredients. The second time he came to town, I decided to sneak in just a bit of garlic and onion, dreading to repeat the previous uninteresting menu. With a great deal of trepidation, I observed him savor his first bite.

Nothing happened: no fierce reaction, no wagging of a chastising finger. Instead, a smile of great satisfaction started to surface over his handsome face. His fork kept digging into his plate of *pasta al pomodoro di Ganzirri,* the southern recipe I had learned to prepare during my Sicilian holidays. He nodded with appreciation at the first bite of my *involtini di pollo,* chicken heavily laced with garlic, onion, and every possible Italian herb.

Nonno GianPaolo not only loved every dish I had prepared for him, but he had noticed nothing except that my food tasted especially scrumptious. *"Patrizia cucina meglio di Emilia!* Patrizia cooks better than Emilia!" he informed his wife, back in Livorno.

"Ma cosa mai hai cucinato? What ever did you cook?" Nonna Valentina was perplexed; she drilled me over the phone to

unearth my secrets. I confessed my sin and it quickly became another family tale. But Nonno never found out about my Machiavellian deviousness. I loved him too much to show him, at the end of his life, how his inflexibility had deprived him of one of life's great pleasures.

ACKNOWLEDGMENTS

I have too many people to be grateful to, people without whom this book would not have been possible. They helped me through these years and believed in me when I doubted. Lydia Forbes, who urged me to write in English, persuading me that "if I wanted it, I could do it." And Marion Abbott Bundy, my unswerving friend, persistent mentor, patient teacher, indefatigable Queen of Commas and Paragraphs, steadfast Executor of Adverbs and Adjectives, who convinced me to show it to Maria Campbell. Maria, who took time to explain the mysterious wonders of the publishing world and helped me, sustained me, and rooted for me. Maria introduced me to Julie Rubenstein, Perfect Agent *par excellence* and enthusiastic friend and supporter. Enter Nan Graham, Editor of All Editors, whose incredible eye and vision shaped my memories into a real book. "Simply write, don't worry. Later, we will cut," she said. Never were words more accurate. . . . And Rica Allannic! Wonderful, amusing, smart Rica, who, often puzzled but never perturbed, took care of secular trees and unweighed large eggs.

My lawyer and great friend and neighbor, Gerry Rosenberg,

who kindly convinced me that legal contracts, after all, are useful tools in life.

And, naturally, Mamma who wholeheartedly helped me, making sure that my recollections were at least based in fact. She searched for names and data, gathering Livorno details and information, providing me with wonderful pictures of our family's past. Zio Marcello and Zia Marilena, who often brought to my attention long-forgotten events and inspired me to write about them.

My family, my patient husband, Kimball, and my children, Assia and Saverio, who empowered me with their trust and unshakable faith.

If this book can be compared to any of my culinary projects, its result will be judged by those who will taste it. I wish to have mixed together all the ingredients in the proper quantities and in the right order. I have tried to fold gently my childhood stories with many family anecdotes. My *tiramisù's* blend of coffee, chocolate, and mascarpone is absolutely nothing without the ethereal air bubbles of the egg whites. I hope I have deployed in writing the same care I exercise when I incorporate all that whipped fluffiness into the smooth, creamy mixture.

✿ My Tiramisù ✿

6 large eggs
7 tablespoons sugar
2 tablespoons finely ground coffee
7 ounces dark chocolate, finely chopped
One 18-ounce container mascarpone cheese
1 cup strong Italian coffee

2 tablespoons dark rum
One 14-ounce package savoiardi cookies or ladyfingers
2 tablespoons unsweetened dark cocoa powder

Separate the eggs, putting the yolks into a large mixing bowl and the whites into the bowl of an electric mixer. Add 6 tablespoons of the sugar to the yolks, and whisk until the mixture is pale yellow and creamy. Stir in the ground coffee, chocolate, and mascarpone.

Beat the egg whites with the mixer until they hold stiff peaks. Gently fold them into the mascarpone mixture.

Line the sides of a 9-inch springform pan with foil. In a small shallow bowl, mix together the brewed coffee, rum, and remaining tablespoon sugar. One by one, dip enough cookies into the coffee mixture to cover the bottom of the cake pan. (It doesn't matter if they crumble; this actually improves the consistency of the final dish.) Take the remaining savoiardi, dip them on just one side, and stand them straight up against the sides of the pan, with the moistened side facing in.

Pour the mascarpone filling into the pan and sprinkle with the cocoa powder. Freeze for at least 6 hours.

Let stand at room temperature for 1 hour before serving. To unmmold, spring open the pan, peel away the foil, and transfer the *tiramisù,* still on the pan base, to a plate. *Ecco fatto!*

Makes 10 servings

About the Author

Born in Livorno, Italy, Patrizia Chen has also lived in Japan. She has been a correspondent for numerous Italian publications and currently resides in New York City and Todi, Italy, with her husband. She has two adult children.

CPSIA information can be obtained at www.ICGtesting.com
Printed in the USA
LVOW110926150212

268773LV00003B/107/A